Microwave Cooking for One

by Marie T. Smith

PELICAN PUBLISHING COMPANY
GRETNA 2017

To my family, Hugh, Tracy, and Leslie, without whose encouragement, support, and sense of humor I could not have written this book

First printing, January 1986
Second printing, June 2002
Third printing, January 2005
Fourth printing, December 2014
Fifth printing, August 2017

Library of Congress Cataloging in Publication Data

Smith, Marie T.
   Microwave cooking for one.

   Includes index.
   1. Microwave cookery. I. Title.
TX832.S48   1985   641.5'882   85-6374

ISBN 9781565546660

Printed in the United States of America

Published by Pelican Publishing Company, Inc.
1000 Burmaster Street, Gretna, Louisiana 70053

CONTENTS

ACKNOWLEDGMENTS

The best way to start anything is to start at the beginning, and for me that is my mother, Elvira Caroselli. All the recipes in this book with the word **Momma** in the title are her recipes. Cooking for twelve people each day gave her enough experience to make her a good cook, but her insatiable curiosity about new dishes and her love of variety are the creative joys she passed on to her children. There is no way I can thank her for what she has given me, but I do hope that it will bring her great pleasure to see her recipes in print.

It would be unfair not to mention my family's favorite dish, Roast Beef with Gravy, without thanking my mother-in-law, Anna Smith, for teaching me how to make gravy with potato water. She has always praised my cooking efforts, and she gave me a big push toward starting to write this book when she went out and bought a microwave oven after I demonstrated some of my recipes to her.

Few people have the talent and the time to check and proofread recipes such as these. I am very fortunate to know such a person and to have her for my sister and best friend. Without the help of my sister Anne Maute, this book would have taken much longer than five years to complete.

There is not room to list the countless others who have provided encouragement and support along the way. But I must give two special thanks to my husband, Hugh, for his complete and continuous support and to my daughter Tracy for the grueling task of typing and proofreading the final drafts.

INTRODUCTION

When a woman finds her children grown and her husband away often on business trips, she continues to cook large meals because practice has become indelible routine. But when I found myself in this situation and cooking for one, I eagerly read all the cookbooks about that subject I could find. However, I never found any recipes in those books that I could use because the portions were always more than I could eat and the food was not appealing. The recipe that amused me most was the one for canned soup. It directed the reader to open a can of soup, put half in a saucepan with half a can of water, and put the rest of the soup into the refrigerator for later use. I imagine that that essential book for serious cooks is being rewritten now that canned soup for one is readily available in stores.

In my search for cooking ideas, I attended a microwave oven demonstration, and there I found my pot of gold at the end of the rainbow. The microwave oven seemed to have all the answers for an individual living alone, on a special diet or any diet, in an individual-oriented household, in a working household, or—last but certainly not least—in a cost-conscious household. This magical invention could satisfy individual food needs and keep the kitchen spotlessly clean as well. Shortly after purchasing my microwave, I cleaned up my conventional oven (the housekeeping job I hated the most) for the last time and have not used or cleaned it since.

I eagerly set about adapting my favorite recipes to the new oven and experimenting with many foods that I had given up cooking at home. The smell of cooking shrimp, cabbage, or liver for myself took away my husband's appetite regardless of what I had cooked for him, so I had been forced to eat these dishes only in restaurants. But so little odor comes from cooking in the microwave oven that odor is no longer a problem. Another problem the microwave eliminates is that of the overheated kitchen that wilts the cook so that he or she collapses at the dining table too uncomfortable to eat.

I've read a number of newspaper articles recently in which the authors of so-called gourmet cookbooks smugly dismiss microwave ovens, saying that they cannot turn out good food. I, on the other hand, have found this to be untrue. All the sauteing that is required in French-style cooking is unnecessary in the microwave; therefore, the dishes it produces are much easier on the digestive system. To prepare onions, green peppers, mushrooms, or other vegetables to be added to a recipe, you need only slice or chop the vegetable onto a paper plate, cover it with a paper towel, and cook it until soft. All the flavor and nutritional value remain in the food, and no additional salt or butter is needed. Favorite dishes that had become indigestible to me as I grew older are now edible again.

As I worked on the recipes, I realized that I was developing a collection of recipes that were cooked totally in the microwave oven, were made from scratch, and required no fancy utensils or extra freezer space. Why not go one step further? I decided to compile my recipes in a book that would also include suggestions on what to do with the ingredients that so often go to waste when preparing small amounts of food. So I set about proving to myself that the microwave oven is really the answer for people who have to cook for one or two, or for a family full of individual tastes.

Anyone who has tried to reduce a recipe to a small amount knows that it is not an easy task, but to double or triple a recipe is a fairly simple feat. I've done the tough reducing job for you already in this book; the easy job of increasing these recipes to two or three or four servings is up to you.

One piece of equipment I did not own but decided was essential for this new method of cooking was a small, inexpensive diet scale. Measuring food by weight and not volume is the best method for microwave cooking because such measurement is exact and because the weight of an ingredient determines the length of time it will take to cook in the microwave. A small onion defies exact measurement; 1 ounce of onion, however, is exact. A cup of sliced carrots can vary in weight according to the carrot's diameter and the thickness of the slices. Since most of these recipes require such small amounts, using exactly 2 ounces of carrots will assure uniform results. With the current emphasis on not wasting energy or food and the continuing popularity of slim waistlines, the diet scale should be an integral part of the new American way of cooking and eating. Therefore, before trying the recipes in this book, please buy a diet scale.

If you have been cooking for many years, no one cookbook will completely change the type of foods or spices you prefer. Once you master a number of dishes designed for cooking in the microwave, you will soon find yourself adapting your favorite recipes to microwave cooking. This cookbook is intended as a workbook to help you in that process and to help beginning cooks as well.

Using different ingredients and even different brands of microwave ovens may require cooking times that are different from the times I've specified. One unique feature of this book is the special space provided that makes it possible for you to substitute the time each step requires in your version of the recipe. It may take more than one attempt for you to perfect the timing of a dish required by your oven and your chosen ingredients, but once you do, you will have the timing written down for whenever you need it. Even if your first attempt at a recipe is a total disaster, the small amount of food wasted will keep the cost of your failed experiment relatively low. (See more on cooking times later in this chapter.)

EQUIPMENT

None of the cookbooks I have read or demonstrations of microwave cooking I have seen have emphasized the point that the shape and size of the utensil in which the food is cooked determines how a recipe will turn out, but I have found this to be the case. Consequently, a person may follow a microwave recipe to the letter with disastrous results because the directions vaguely stated, "Cook in a one-quart casserole."

In order to prepare a recipe properly in a microwave oven, the utensil recommended in the cookbook should be used. If a different utensil is used and the recipe is followed faithfully but the results are poor, the failure can be attributed to the cooking utensil. You may safely substitute other utensils if the sizes and shapes are the same. If you have not yet acquired many cooking utensils, you can cook most of the recipes in the book with three basic utensils: the 1½-pint Menu-ette, the 1-quart Cook 'N' Pour Pan, and the 6″ browning skillet.

All liquid and dry ingredients should be measured in metal measuring cups, which are usually used only for dry measurements. The glass measuring cups normally used for liquid measurement allow too much variation in amounts, producing variations in results. In addition, the markings on glass measuring cups wear off with frequent use.

As I mentioned before, a diet scale is essential in preparing the recipes in this book. Some of these scales come with a plastic tray that makes them easier to use. As an added feature, the tray can be put right into the oven to hold frozen food during defrosting. However, **do not cook food in the tray.**

Used extensively throughout the book, finger tongs are a safe and easy way to add food to hot browning dishes in the oven and arrange and turn over hot food. No other utensil gives you the control needed in such a confined area.

The next section lists the utensils called for in these recipes and their manufacturers. Only one plastic utensil—a plastic strainer—is listed. I have found that plastic cooking utensils are too fragile and too difficult to clean; in addition, the food they produce just doesn't taste as good as the food produced by ceramic or glass dishes. To clean any food encrusted on ceramic or glass utensils, put a small amount of dishwasher detergent in the utensil, add hot water, and allow to soak for a half hour. The utensil will rinse clean, and your kitchen cleanup time will be reduced considerably.

EQUIPMENT LIST

Corning Ware:

Baking Dish, 1½-quart (7½" x 6" x 3¼")

Browning utensils: Microwave Browning Griddle, Browning Grill, Microwave Pizza Crisper (12"), Browning Skillets (6", 8½", 10")

Casser-ette, 14-oz.

Casseroles, 1-quart, 1½-quart

Cook 'N' Pour Pan

Covered Cooker with Built-in Rack (10") or 2½-quart Oval Roaster with Built-in Rack

Gravy Maker Pot, 1-quart

Menu-ettes, 1-pint, 1½-pint

Menu-ette Skillet

Petite Pan, 16-oz.

Pie plate (9")

Pots, 1-quart, 1½-quart, 3-quart, 5-quart

Bowls:

Cereal bowls

Mixing bowls, 1½-pint, 1-quart, 1½-quart, 2-quart

Pyrex Bake Mate (straight-sided storage bowl), 14-oz.

Assorted shallow bowls

Assorted small bowls

Cups:

Pfaltzgraff ceramic measuring cups with handles, ½-cup, 1-cup

Custard cups, ceramic and glass

Irish coffee mug

Dishes:

Pyrex refrigerator dish, 1½-cup

Pillivuyt ceramic souffle dish, 16-oz.

Pyrex souffle dish, 24-oz.

Pillivuyt ceramic souffle dish, 48-oz.

Ovenware: Liquid measure, 1-cup, 2-cup

Plates: Pyrex pie plate (6″)
El Camino ceramic plate with handles (11″)

Utensils·   Blender
Brushes, basting and mushroom
Cutting board (dishwasher-safe)
Diet scale
Electric mixer
Fancy ramekins
Forks, large, small, regular, and two-tined
Jar with lid, small
Kitchen shears
Knife, serrated
Magic Mop
Measuring spoons
Meat pounder
Metal measuring cups
Microwave plastic dome cover
Mortar and pestle
Pancake turners, regular and slotted
Paper plates
Paper towels
Parchment paper
Pastry blender
Pie weights, ceramic
Plastic bags, 1-gallon
Plastic cooking bags, 24-oz.
Plastic freezer containers
Plastic sandwich bags
Plastic wrap
Potato masher
Spatulas, rubber and small metal
Spoon, slotted
Strainers, plastic and small metal
Thermometer, microwave
Tongs, finger, long, and regular
Waxed paper
Wire whisks, regular and small

INGREDIENTS

How often have you denied yourself a dish of chocolate pudding because you did not want to make and eat the whole box? You can have that pudding—along with the chocolate cake, the custard, and many of the other delights you have been denying yourself. Now these recipes are practical for the person cooking for one. All of the ingredients used in this book are available in local food stores, not just in specialty shops.

Incorporated into the index are listings of ingredients that do not store well if left over and of unusual ingredients that you may not have many uses for. For example, if you have a pound of ground beef (which is usually the smallest amount you can buy), the index can show you how to cook four ounces of it a different way each day for the next four days. A prepackaged carton of blueberries or strawberries can be used in a recipe and the rest cooked up into preserves; a carton of mushrooms can be used in many recipes during the week or all at once in the Mushroom Loaf recipe in the Vegetables section.

Most cities have at least one supermarket that does not package all of its fresh produce, so selections of small amounts and uniform shapes and sizes can be made. When writing my shopping list, I note the weights of the ingredients I need so that I will only buy enough food to make a dish. This cuts down considerably on food costs and the throwing away of spoiled food and leftovers. Many supermarkets will undo a package of produce on request and measure out a certain amount. Every supermarket butcher I have ever dealt with has cheerfully reduced the amount of meat in a package in the meat case if I requested it. However, society's changes are helping the customer; as the number of single-occupant homes in this country continues to increase, the food industry must gear its packaging more and more for the individual consumer.

Here are some hints on how to use and store perishable ingredients without wasting them:

Bacon: To store bacon, wrap each slice in a piece of waxed paper, then wrap all the slices tightly in freezer wrap and place in freezer. Remove each slice as needed and add to recipe frozen.

Butter: Butter is an optional ingredient in many of these recipes, but it does enhance the taste of a dish. Margarine may be substituted for butter in each case.

Carrots: Frozen carrots cook better in soups than fresh carrots do. Cut frozen carrot slices in quarters or use the small carrot cubes found in packages of frozen mixed vegetables.

Celery: Keeps well in the crisper drawer of the refrigerator. Do not eliminate it when it is called for in recipes.

Eggs: There are roughly 2 tablespoons of egg in a small egg and 4 tablespoons in an extra-large egg. You may want to keep a box of extra-large eggs on hand if you have one each day for breakfast, but otherwise, small eggs will do for most of these recipes.

Frozen vegetables: Today almost any vegetable you might need is available frozen in bags. This makes it easy and practical to use the exact amount of vegetables needed and return the rest to the freezer.

Garlic: Most of the recipes in this book call for 1/8 teaspoon of garlic. Mince the whole clove and measure out what you need. Spread the rest on a small piece of waxed paper, fold the paper into a small square, put it into a small plastic container, and freeze it. When using the frozen garlic, check its color; if it doesn't look the same as it did before freezing, don't use it. If you use garlic often, mince several cloves at one time and store it the same way.

Green peppers: Use the amount needed for a recipe, cut the rest of the pepper into chunks, and put it into a small plastic container. Frozen green pepper will keep quite a while and is easily chopped, minced, or sliced. Add it frozen to recipes.

Ground beef:

Divide the beef into 2-ounce portions. Place each portion in a plastic sandwich bag and press flat. Put into a square heavy plastic container with the newest meat on the bottom; use the oldest meat on the top first. If a recipe calls for one ounce of beef, break the package into two 1-ounce sections.

Mozzarella cheese:

Quality-brand bulk packages of cheese freeze best. After opening a new package, freeze the leftover cheese in a plastic bag and grate it frozen as you need it.

Onions:

Chopped white onions are used in these recipes. Chop up several onions at a time, freeze them in a plastic container, and add them to the recipes frozen. Frozen chopped onion can be minced easily.

Parsley:

Fresh parsley adds to the flavor of a dish and freezes well. It is sold in bunches, so chop the entire bunch, put it into a plastic container, and freeze.

Potatoes:

Except for Potato Salad and Parslied Potatoes, all recipes call for baking potatoes.

Salt:

Many of these recipes do not require any salt. The microwave oven emphasizes the salt content of food, so recipes containing a conventional amount of salt will taste twice as salty. Canned vegetables, cheese, bacon, and other such ingredients already contain enough salt and can be cooked in the microwave oven without added salt.

Sausage: Italian sausage freezes better in one piece. In its frozen state, it is easily cut and skinned, but it tastes better if it is defrosted before being added to a recipe.

Tomatoes (fresh): You can use cherry tomatoes in most recipes requiring fresh tomatoes. Because of their size, it is easy to use the exact amount needed in a recipe and store the unused portion for a long time in the refrigerator.

Tomato paste: Most of the recipes call for 1 tablespoon of tomato paste, but the rest of the can freezes well in a small plastic container and, when frozen, is easy to cut with a dull kitchen knife.

Tomato sauce: Many recipes call for 4 ounces of tomato sauce or less, which is less than a small can. The unused portion won't store for more than a week in a jar in the refrigerator, but there are 17 recipes in which it can be used.

TIMING

The manual that comes with each microwave oven includes all the charts and listings for timing various foods in that oven; they should be studied and followed carefully. This section covers only the timing of the recipes I've included in this book.

The length of time it takes to cook a dish is of critical importance in a microwave oven, and the smaller the amount of food being prepared, the more precise the timing must be. A few seconds can mean the difference between total disaster and delicious success. Since no two ovens are identical, it is essential to have a place to pencil in the time it took for each step in your oven when trying a new recipe. (Pencil is best because a change of any kind—moving to a new location, using different brands of food, changing utensils—may change the timing.) Therefore, following each recommended time in these recipes is a blank line on which to jot down the exact time each procedure takes in your oven.

At the end of most recipes you will find instructions to let the food stand for a few minutes. Your microwave oven manual should explain how food continues to cook after it is taken out of the oven. Manufacturers call this standing time, holding time, or resting time, but it is actually residual cooking time, and it is a very important part of microwave cooking. It allows the food to finish cooking and gives the flavors time to blend, thereby improving the taste of the food.

All the recipes in this book can be cooked in a simple 700-watt oven with 100%, 50%, and 30% power settings; they do not require a more sophisticated oven. To assure accuracy, the recipes were tested in an autorotating oven with a probe and ten power settings. If a difference in time or procedure is required for different types of ovens, the recipe will say so; otherwise, the times listed apply to all ovens. In general, when doubling a recipe, double the cooking time; exceptions are noted in the recipes.

In microwave cooking, dishes are cooked one at a time, set aside, then popped back into the oven individually just before serving until piping hot. I have found that cooking dishes in a particular order gets the best results. I cook starchy vegetables first, green or yellow vegetables second, and meat, fish, or poultry last. To refer back to recipes I cook as a meal, I use 3 bookmarks labeled 1—starchy vegetable, 2—green vegetable, and 3—meat or fish. I suggest you make bookmarks of your own and use them for ready reference.

SPECIAL TIPS

Know the wattage of your oven. Most published recipes are for 700-watt ovens, so if yours is less than 700 watts, learn how to increase cooking times.

When you try a new recipe, jot down the results right on the recipe so that next time you will know the changes or adjustments you need to make.

Cook frozen foods while still frozen unless a recipe gives directions for defrosting.

Use only plain white paper towels and use them carefully. Don't put one in an empty hot browning dish or place the hot dish on one.

Remove plastic wrap carefully from hot food. Lift up the farthest edge and pull it toward you so the steam will be released away from you.

Use metal measuring cups for both liquid and dry measurements.

You do not have to buy a lot of new utensils. You can cook most of the recipes in this book with three basic utensils: a 1½-pint Menu-ette, a 1-quart Cook 'N' Pour Pan, and a 6″ browning skillet.

Learn to use browning utensils properly. Leave the heated utensil in the oven between cooking steps: it is safer, and heat is not lost by carrying the utensil back and forth.

BREAKFAST

HOT CEREAL

1 cup cold cereal (cereal
    usually eaten cold, such
    as bran flakes)
1 tbsp. sugar
3/4 cup milk

Put all ingredients into cereal bowl. Cook
30 seconds (_____) **at 100% power.** Serve in cereal bowl.

OATMEAL

1/3 cup quick-cooking oatmeal
pinch of salt
1/3 cup water
sugar and milk to taste

Place ingredients in cereal bowl or 1-pint
Menu-ette. Cook **1 minute** (_____)
at 100% power. Mixture will be thick.
Stir well with spoon. Add sugar and
milk. Serve in cereal bowl.

CREAM OF WHEAT

2 tbsp. Cream of Wheat
dash of salt
1/2 cup milk or water
sugar to taste

Put ingredients in the order listed into
1½-pint Menu-ette.* Cook **1 minute**
(_____) **at 100% power.** Stir well
with fork. Cook **45 seconds** (_____)
at 100% power. Add sugar and stir. If
mixture is too watery, let stand **1 minute** (_____).

milk or cream to taste

Add milk and stir. Serve in Menu-ette.

* In an autorotating oven, Cream of Wheat cooked with milk may boil over in
Menu-ette. Use a deeper utensil such as a Cook 'N' Pour Pan, Gravy Maker
Pot, or 1-quart mixing bowl.

GRITS

3/4 cup water
1/8 tsp. salt
3 tbsp. regular grits*

Pour water into Cook 'N' Pour Pan or Gravy Maker Pot. Cook **2 minutes** (_____) **at 100% power** until water boils. Add salt and stir in grits. Cover pan with lid. Cook **2 minutes** (_____) **at 100% power.** Let stand **2 minutes** (_____).

1 tbsp. instant nonfat dry
   milk (optional)**
1 tsp. butter

Stir in milk until well blended. Add butter and mix well before serving.

 * Quick grits can be substituted in this recipe, but regular grits taste better.
** Instant milk increases the nutritional value.

STEWED PRUNES

2 oz. dry prunes with pits
2 tbsp. water

Put prunes and water into Menu-ette. Cover with lid. Cook **1:30 minutes** (_____) **at 100% power.** Let stand **5 minutes** (_____) until cool enough to eat.

If moist, plump prunes are preferred, cook prunes the night before and put covered Menu-ette into refrigerator. To heat before serving, cook **30 seconds** (_____) **at 100% power.**

FLAKY HOMEMADE BISCUITS

1/2 cup all-purpose flour
1½ tsp. baking powder
1/8 tsp. salt
1/8 tsp. baking soda
1½ tbsp. butter

Mix dry ingredients with fork in 1-quart mixing bowl. Using pastry blender, cut in butter until mixture resembles coarse crumbs. Set aside.

1 tsp. white vinegar
3 tbsp. milk

Mix vinegar and milk in custard cup and add to dry mixture. Stir with fork until ingredients are moistened and dough clings together. With rubber spatula, scrape dough onto floured paper plate and knead gently 4 or 5 turns. Pat dough into a circle 5 inches wide and 1 inch thick. With floured 2" biscuit cutter or empty small can, cut out 3 biscuits, making the cuts straight down and as close together as possible. Gently push out each biscuit onto a floured paper plate as it is cut. Pat scraps together and shape fourth biscuit. Leave on plate and set aside.

Heat 10" browning skillet **2:30 minutes (_____) at 100% power.** Arrange biscuits in center of skillet. Cook **1 minute (_____) at 100% power.** Turn biscuits over with finger tongs. Cook **1 minute (_____) at 100% power** until sides of biscuits are dry. Wrap in paper towel and let stand **3 minutes (_____)** before serving.

REFRIGERATOR BISCUITS

Note: There are two major types of refrigerator biscuits available. Read label directions carefully before selecting one of these cooking methods. If directions read "Place in greased pan," follow method 1. If directions read "Place in ungreased pan," follow method 2.

Method 1:

5-oz. can flaky biscuits (can size may vary slightly)

1 tsp. vegetable oil or melted butter

Place biscuits on paper plate. Spread half the oil on one side of biscuits and set aside. Heat 10" browning skillet **2 minutes (_____) at 100% power.** Arrange biscuits, greased side down, in skillet. Cook **50 seconds (_____) at 100% power.** Spread remaining oil on biscuits and turn biscuits over. Cook **30 seconds (_____) at 100% power.** Sides of biscuits should be dry. Wrap in paper towel and let stand **3 minutes (_____)** before serving.

Method 2:

6-oz. can butter-flavored biscuits or baking powder biscuits (can size may vary slightly)

Follow directions for method 1, but do not grease biscuits.

CINNAMON TOAST

2 tsp. sugar
1/4 tsp. cinnamon

Mix sugar and cinnamon in custard cup and set aside.

2 slices white bread, toasted

Put toasted bread on plate and set aside.

1 tbsp. butter

Put butter into another custard cup. Cook **15 seconds (_____) at 100% power** until melted. Brush butter liberally on one side of each slice of toast. **Sprinkle cinnamon and sugar mixture over butter. Cut toast diagonally into halves** and serve.

FRENCH TOAST

1 extra-large egg or
   2 small eggs
dash of salt
1 tbsp. sugar
1/2 tsp. vanilla
2 tbsp. milk*

Put egg, salt, sugar, vanilla, and milk into Menu-ette Skillet or other shallow dish. Mix well with wire whisk or fork.

3 or 4 slices of Pepperidge Farm Toasting White Bread or any small white bread

Heat 10" browning skillet **4 minutes (_____) at 100% power.** While skillet is heating, dip bread into egg mixture one slice at a time until all slices are coated. Set bread aside in dish.

1 tbsp. butter

Divide butter into quarters. Pick up a piece of butter with one hand and a slice of bread with the other. Quickly put butter into one corner of skillet and cover it with a slice of bread. Repeat for remaining slices of bread. Cook **30 seconds (_____) at 100% power.** Turn bread over with pancake turner. Cook **1 minute (_____) at 100% power.**

honey, syrup, or
   cinnamon sugar

Put bread on plate and cover with desired topping

* If egg mixture is not sufficient to coat the bread used, add more milk to mixture.

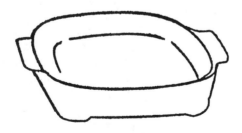

BUTTERMILK PANCAKES

Basic ingredients:

1/4 cup all-purpose flour
1/8 tsp. baking soda
1/4 tsp. baking powder
1/4 tsp. sugar
1/2 tsp. salt

Put dry ingredients into 1-quart mixing bowl. Mix well with wire whisk.

Directions using pizza crisper:

1 small egg
1/4 cup buttermilk
1 tbsp. vegetable oil

Add remaining ingredients and mix with wire whisk. Heat pizza crisper **4 minutes (_____) at 100% power.** Near center of crisper ladle batter to make 3 5-inch pancakes (about 3 heaping spoonfuls each). Cook **1 minute (_____) at 100% power.** Flip pancakes over with pancake turner. Cook **15 seconds (_____) at 100% power.**

butter
honey or syrup

Stack pancakes on plate. Serve with butter and honey or syrup.

Directions using 10" browning skillet:

pat of butter

Heat skillet **1:30 minutes (_____) at 100% power.** Quickly and lightly coat bottom of skillet with pat of butter. Pour batter into skillet and carefully spread out with rubber spatula to cover skillet evenly. Hold skillet by handles and tilt gently in all directions to even out batter. Cook **3 minutes (_____) at 100% power,** giving skillet a half-turn halfway through cooking time. (Autorotating oven: Cook **2 minutes (_____) at 100% power,** eliminating turn.)

butter
honey or syrup

Cut pancake into quarters with edge of pancake turner. Lay one quarter on plate with browned side up. Top with small amount of butter and some honey or syrup. Do the same with remaining quarters, topping each with butter and honey or syrup.

LESLIE'S FAVORITE GRIDDLE CAKES

1 tsp. butter
1/2 cup all-purpose flour
1/2 tsp. baking powder
1/2 tsp. sugar
1/8 tsp. salt (optional)

Put butter into 1-quart mixing bowl. Cook **20 seconds (_____) at 100% power.** Stir with wire whisk until butter is creamy. Add dry ingredients to butter and mix well with whisk.

1 small egg
1/4 cup milk
2 tsp. vegetable oil

Add remaining ingredients and mix with whisk until blended. Heat pizza crisper* **4 minutes (_____) at 100% power.** Near center of crisper ladle batter into 3 equal portions (about 2 heaping spoonfuls each). With rubber spatula flatten each portion into a 5-inch pancake. Cook **1:15 minutes (_____) at 100% power.** Flip each pancake over with pancake turner. Cook **15 seconds (_____) at 100% power.**

butter
honey or syrup

Stack pancakes on plate. Serve with butter and honey or syrup.

* For directions using 10″ browning skillet, see recipe for Buttermilk Pancakes.

WHOLE-WHEAT PANCAKES

1/4 cup whole-wheat flour
1/4 cup corn flake crumbs
4 tsp. wheat germ
1/8 tsp. baking soda

Put dry ingredients into 1-quart mixing bowl and mix with wire whisk.

1 small egg
1/4 cup buttermilk or
  sour milk*
1 tbsp. hot water
1 tbsp. vegetable oil
1 tbsp. honey

Add remaining ingredients and mix with wire whisk just until blended. Heat pizza crisper** 4 minutes (_____) at 100% power. Ladle out batter into 3 portions near center of crisper with rubber spatula. Flatten each portion into a 5-inch pancake. Cook **1:30 minutes** (_____) **at 100% power.** Flip pancakes over with pancake turner. Cook 15 seconds (_____) at 100% power.

butter
honey or syrup

Stack pancakes on plate. Serve with butter and honey or syrup.

 * To sour milk, put 1 tsp. vinegar into a measuring cup and add milk to make 1/4 cup.
** For directions using 10″ browning skillet, see recipe for Buttermilk Pancakes.

SOFT-BOILED EGG

Note: Prepare this first and cook the rest of the meal while the egg is standing in water.

2 cups water

Pour water into 1-quart mixing bowl. Cook **5 minutes** (_____) **at 100% power** until water boils.

1 extra-large egg

Place egg on counter while water boils. Carefully pick up egg with tongs and place in water. Cover bowl with plate and let stand **15 minutes** (_____). Pour off hot water and add cold water to stop cooking action. Remove egg from water and serve in eggcup.

SUNNY-SIDE-UP EGG

pat of butter

Heat 6″ browning skillet **45 seconds** (_____) **at 100% power.** Put skillet on counter and quickly run butter over bottom of skillet to lightly coat it.

1 extra-large egg or
2 small eggs
pinch of salt (optional)
about 1 tsp. water

Break egg into skillet. Sprinkle salt on top of egg yolk. Sprinkle water on top of egg. Cover skillet with lid. Cook **45 seconds** (_____) **at 100% power.** (There may be a popping sound when the membrane pops, so do not be alarmed.) If a small amount of egg white is still transparent immediately after cooking, leave lid in place and allow skillet to stand for **10 seconds** (_____) until it is opaque. If a large amount of egg white is still transparent, return skillet to oven and cook **5 seconds** (_____) **at 100% power.** Remove egg from skillet with slotted turner and place on plate. Serve immediately.

EGG OVER EASY

Follow recipe for Sunny-Side-Up Egg except sprinkle with salt after egg is cooked and cover skillet with paper towel, not water and a lid. Cook **35 seconds** (_____) **at 100% power,** turn egg over with turner, and let stand in skillet **5 seconds** (_____) before placing on plate.

SCRAMBLED EGGS

1 extra-large egg or
  2 small eggs
2 tsp. milk
pinch of salt
pinch of black pepper
1/2 tsp. butter (optional)

Break egg into 1-quart mixing bowl. Add milk, salt, and pepper. Beat well with wire whisk. Add butter to mixture. Cook **1 minute (_____) at 100% power** until about 1 tbsp. of egg remains uncooked. Mix egg well with rubber spatula and serve. Egg will be moist; if dry eggs are preferred, cook **5 seconds (_____) more at 100% power** until all the egg is cooked. Mix with rubber spatula and serve.

EGG PARMESAN

1 tsp. dry bread crumbs
1 tbsp. sour cream

Put bread crumbs into 1-cup ceramic measuring cup with handle. Carefully spoon sour cream on top and spread evenly over bread crumbs with small fork.

1 extra-large egg or
  2 small eggs
1 tsp. butter, divided
  into quarters
1 tbsp. sour cream

Break egg into cup and puncture egg yolk with fork. Place butter on top of egg, spacing evenly around yolk. With a knife, put small dollops of sour cream around inside edge of cup to surround egg entirely.

1 tsp. dry bread crumbs
1 tsp. grated Parmesan or
  Parmesan/Romano cheese

Sprinkle top with bread crumbs. Sprinkle cheese on top of bread crumbs. Cook **50 seconds (_____) at 100% power.** Serve in cup.

POACHED EGG ON TOAST

1/2 cup water

Pour water into 1-pint Menu-ette. Cook **1:15 minutes (_____) at 100% power** until water boils.

butter
1 extra-large egg or
  2 small eggs

Butter inside of custard cup. Break egg into cup. Puncture egg yolk with fork. Put cup into Menu-ette and cover with lid. Cook **1:10 minutes (_____) at 100% power,** giving Menu-ette a half-turn halfway through cooking time. (Autorotating oven: Cook **1 minute (_____) at 100% power,** eliminating turn.)

pinch of salt
pinch of black pepper

Remove cup from Menu-ette. Sprinkle with salt and pepper. Loosen egg from cup with a dull knife.

1 slice toasted bread

Put toast on plate. Turn cup upside down on top of toast so egg unmolds on toast and serve.

HAM AND EGGS

1 tsp. butter
1 tbsp. (1 oz.) chopped
  cooked ham

Put butter and ham into Menu-ette Skillet. Cover skillet with paper towel. Cook **1 minute (_____) at 100% power.**

1 extra-large egg or
  2 small eggs
1 tbsp. milk
pinch of salt
pinch of black pepper

Put remaining ingredients into 1-quart mixing bowl. Beat well with wire whisk. Pour mixture into Menu-ette. Cook **55 seconds (_____) at 100% power** until about 1 tbsp. of egg remains uncooked. Mix well with rubber spatula and serve.

BACON

Note: To collect bacon drippings, cook bacon in a dish with a rack. Cover bacon with paper towel to prevent splattering.

To cook 2 or 3 slices bacon:

Place paper towel on paper plate and lay bacon on top. Cover with another paper towel. Cook **1:45 minutes (_____) at 100% power** for 2 slices or **2:40 minutes (_____) at 100% power** for 3 slices until bacon is well done. Drain on paper towel before serving.

To cook 4 slices bacon:

Place paper towel on paper plate and lay 2 slices bacon on top. Cover with a second paper towel. Lay remaining 2 slices bacon on top of that and cover with a third paper towel. Cook **3:30 minutes (_____) at 100% power** until well done. Drain on paper towel before serving.

To cook 1 lb. bacon:

Place paper towel on paper plate and lay 3 slices bacon on top. Cover with a second paper towel. Lay next 3 slices on top, cover with another paper towel, and continue layering remaining bacon 3 slices at a time. (A paper towel cannot absorb the grease from more than 3 slices bacon. Putting more slices in a layer will cause excess grease to ooze out onto bottom of oven.) Cook **15 minutes (_____) at 100% power** until well done. It is better to undercook bacon at first and check as additional cooking time progresses than to try to salvage a pound of overcooked bacon.

FRESH SAUSAGE PATTIE

Note: To double recipe, use 10″ browning skillet and heat **4 minutes** (_____) **at 100% power.** Double cooking time.

4 oz. fresh bulk sausage

Heat 8½″ browning skillet **4 minutes** (_____) **at 100% power.** Cut a 12-inch piece of waxed paper. Divide sausage into two portions and place both portions on one half of waxed paper. Cover with other half of waxed paper and flatten into two 4-inch patties with palm of hand.

Place sausage in skillet and cover skillet with paper towel. Cook **30 seconds at 100% power.** Turn sausage over. Cook **1 minute** (_____) **at 100% power.** Drain on paper towel for **1 minute** (_____) and serve.

FRESH LINK SAUSAGE

4 oz. (4 links) fresh pork breakfast sausage

Heat 6″ browning skillet **4 minutes** (_____) **at 100% power.** Place sausage in skillet and cover with paper towel. Cook **1:45 minutes** (_____) **at 100% power,** turning sausage 3 times during cooking to brown sides evenly. Drain on paper towel for **1 minute** (_____) and serve.

SMOKED COUNTRY SAUSAGE

2½ oz. smoked country
sausage

Place 2 paper towels on paper plate. Cut sausage into four links and place on top of paper towels. Cover with another paper towel. Cook **1 minute** (_____) **at 100% power.** Drain sausage on paper towel and serve.

FULLY COOKED FROZEN SAUSAGE

3 oz. frozen fully cooked
link or pattie sausage
1/4 tsp. Kitchen Bouquet
(optional)

Place paper towel on paper plate and place sausage on top of paper towel. Spread Kitchen Bouquet over sausage. Defrost **2 minutes** (_____) **at 30% power,** then spread Kitchen Bouquet more evenly over sausage. Cook **45 seconds** (_____) **at 100% power.** Let stand **1 minute** (_____) before serving.

SOUPS

ASPARAGUS SOUP

1/2 cup chicken stock (see recipe) or 1/2 cup water with 1 chicken bouillon cube

Put stock into 1-cup liquid measure. Cook **1 minute (_____) at 100% power.** Pour into blender and set aside.

1 tsp. butter
1 tbsp. chopped fresh or frozen onion

Put butter and onion into Gravy Maker Pot or Cook 'N' Pour Pan. Cook **1 minute (_____) at 100% power.**

3 oz. (6 spears) fresh or frozen asparagus

Cut asparagus into 1-inch pieces. Add to onion mixture and cover pot with lid. Cook **2 minutes (_____) at 100% power.** Set aside asparagus tips in emptied liquid measure. Pour remaining mixture into blender.

1 tsp. all-purpose flour
dash of salt
dash of black pepper
3 tbsp. half and half

Add remaining ingredients to blender. Liquify contents, then pour back into pot. Add asparagus tips and cover with lid. Cook **1:30 minutes (_____) at 100% power.** Pour into soup bowl and serve.

CARROT SOUP

1/2 tbsp. butter
2 tbsp. chopped fresh or
frozen onion
1 cup chicken stock (see
recipe) or 1 cup water
with 1 chicken bouillon
cube
1/2 tsp. sugar
4 oz. sliced fresh or
frozen carrots

Put butter and onion into Gravy Maker Pot. Cook **1 minute** (_____) at **100% power.** Add stock, sugar, and carrots. Cover pot with lid. Cook **2 minutes** (_____) at **100% power.** Stir. Cook **8 minutes** (_____) at **50% power.**

1/16 tsp. salt
pinch of cinnamon
pinch of nutmeg

Pour contents of pot into blender. Add salt, cinnamon, and nutmeg to blender and liquify. Pour into soup bowl and serve.

CHEESE SOUP

1 tbsp. butter
1/8 tsp. minced fresh or
frozen garlic

Place butter and garlic in 1½-pint Menuette. Cook **45 seconds** (_____) at **100% power.**

1 tbsp. all-purpose flour
1/2 cup half and half

Add flour and mix with wire whisk. Add half and half and mix well with whisk. Cook **1 minute** (_____) at **100% power** until mixture boils.

2 oz. grated sharp cheddar
cheese
1/16 tsp. white pepper
few grains of nutmeg

Add cheese, pepper, and nutmeg and mix with whisk. Cook **30 seconds at 100% power.**

2 tbsp. Chablis or other
dry white wine

Add wine and mix carefully with whisk. Cook **30 seconds** (_____) at **100% power.** Pour into soup bowl and serve.

Variation: Crumble 1 slice of cooked bacon and sprinkle on top of soup.

CHICKEN STOCK

8 oz. chicken with skin
  and bone
1 cup water
1/2 tsp. salt
2 peppercorns
2 oz. carrots, cut into
  1-inch pieces
1 oz. celery, cut into
  1-inch pieces
small garlic clove (optional)

Wash chicken and put into 1-quart mixing bowl. Add remaining ingredients. Cook **5 minutes (_____) at 100% power** until mixture boils. Skim off and discard scum. Cook stock **20 minutes (_____) at 50% power.** Strain liquid into clean container* and refrigerate until fat solidifies. Scrape off and discard solid fat.

To freeze stock for future use, pour into ice cube tray, freeze, and store cubes in plastic bag. Add to soups and gravies or serve as is: Put 6 cubes in Menu-ette and cover with lid. Cook **2 minutes (_____) at 100% power.** Pour into soup mug and serve.

* After straining stock, save carrots and chicken and discard remaining contents of strainer. Add carrots and chicken to stock to make chicken soup.

CUCUMBER SOUP

1 tsp. butter
1 tbsp. chopped fresh or
  frozen onion

Place butter and onion in 1½-pint Menu-ette. Cook **1 minute (_____) at 100% power.** Set aside.

4-oz. unpeeled cucumber

Wash and chop cucumber into 1-inch cubes. Add to Menu-ette and cover with lid. Cook **2 minutes (_____) at 100% power.**

1/3 cup chicken stock (see recipe) or 1/3 cup water with 1/2 chicken bouillon cube

Put stock into blender and add contents of Menu-ette. Liquify.

dash of salt
dash of black pepper
3 tbsp. half and half

Pour contents of blender back into Menu-ette and add remaining ingredients. Cook **2 minutes (_____) at 100% power.** Stir, pour into soup bowl, and serve.

MOMMA'S ESCAROLE SOUP

3 oz. chicken with skin and bone (1 thigh will do)

Wash chicken and put into 1½-pint Menu-ette. Cover with lid. Cook **2 minutes (_____) at 100% power.** Place chicken on plate to cool.

2 oz. escarole

Wash escarole and chop into 1-inch pieces. Place in Menu-ette and cover with lid. Cook **2 minutes (_____) at 100% power.** Remove escarole and place on plate with chicken, leaving liquid in Menu-ette.

3/4 cup water or 6 frozen cubes chicken stock (see recipe)
1/8 tsp. salt
2 oz. carrots, cut in 1/2-inch pieces
1 oz. sliced celery

Add water, salt, carrots, and celery to Menu-ette. Cover with lid. Cook **8 minutes (_____) at 100% power.**

1/2 chicken bouillon cube
1/4 cup water or 2 frozen cubes chicken stock (see recipe)

While liquid cooks, remove skin and bones from chicken and cut into 1-inch pieces. Remove celery from liquid after cooking and discard. Add bouillon and water to liquid and mix well. Add chicken and escarole. Cover with lid. Cook **1 minute (_____) at 100% power.** Pour into soup bowl and serve.

FISH CHOWDER

2 tbsp. chopped fresh or
  frozen onion
1 tsp. butter
1/2 cup water
1/4 chicken bouillon cube
3-oz. baking potato, cut into
  1/2-inch cubes
1/4 tsp. dill seed
1/4 tsp. salt
1/8 tsp. black pepper

Put onion and butter into 1½-pint Menu-ette. Cook **1 minute** (_____) **at 100% power.** Add water, bouillon, potato and spices. Cover Menu-ette with lid. Cook **4 minutes** (_____) **at 100% power.**

1/4 cup fresh or frozen
  green beans, cut into
  1/2-inch pieces

Add green beans. Cover with lid. Cook **2 minutes** (_____) **at 100% power.**

3-oz. fresh or frozen fish
  fillet, cut into 1-inch
  pieces

Add fish to Menu-ette and cover with lid. Cook **3 minutes** (_____) **at 100% power.**

2 tbsp. sour cream
1/2 tsp. dried parsley or
  1½ tsp. chopped fresh
  or frozen parsley

Add sour cream and stir. Cover with lid. Cook **20 seconds** (_____) **at 100% power.** Add parsley. Let stand covered **1 minute** (_____) and serve.

OXTAIL SOUP

1/2 tsp. butter

Place butter into small paper cup or custard cup. Cook **20 seconds** (_____) **at 100% power** to soften.

5 to 7 oz. beef oxtails

Lay oxtails on a piece of waxed paper. Spread or brush butter on one side of each oxtail and set aside.

Heat 6″ browning skillet **3 minutes** (_____) **at 100% power.** Place oxtails buttered side down in skillet. Cover with microwave plastic dome cover. Cook **2 minutes** (_____) **at 100% power,** turning oxtails over halfway through cooking time to brown both sides. Put oxtails and juice into Gravy Maker Pot and set aside.

2 tbsp. water

Pour water into skillet. Cook **30 seconds** (_____) **at 100% power.** Pour into pot.

3/4 cup water or beef stock
1 tbsp. chopped fresh or frozen onion
2 tsp. medium pearled barley

Add water, onion, and barley to pot. Liquid should almost cover oxtails. Cover pot with lid. Cook **2 minutes** (_____) **at 100% power** until mixture boils. Cook **15 minutes** (_____) **at 30% power.**

1/4 cup (1 oz.) fresh or frozen peas
1 oz. fresh or frozen carrots
1/2 oz. sliced celery

Add vegetables. Replace lid. Cook **3 minutes** (_____) **at 100% power.** Remove solids with slotted spoon and place in empty skillet. Put pot into freezer to solidify fat. Meanwhile, remove meat from oxtails and discard fat and bones. Remove pot from freezer. Skim off and discard solid fat.*

1 tbsp. dry white wine	Add wine, salt, and Kitchen Bouquet to
1/8 tsp. salt	pot and stir. Put vegetables and meat
1/8 tsp. Kitchen Bouquet	back into pot and cover with lid. Cook
	2 minutes (_____) at 100% pow-
	er until soup is heated. Pour into soup
	bowl and serve.

* If fat is not solid, cover surface of liquid with ice cubes for several minutes.
  Discard solidified fat and ice cubes.

PEA SOUP

1 cup (4½ oz.) frozen peas or 1 cup fresh peas (1 lb. unshelled)	Place peas and water into 1½-pint Menu-ette. Cover with lid. Cook **3 min-utes (_____) at 100% power.** Pour
1 tbsp. water	into blender.
1 tbsp. butter	Put butter, carrots, and onion into emp-
2 oz. frozen carrots	ty Menu-ette. Cover with lid. Cook **2**
2 tbsp. chopped fresh or frozen onion	**minutes (_____) at 100% power.** Add to blender. Add stock and spices
3/4 cup chicken stock (see recipe) or 3/4 cup water with 1 chicken bouillon cube	to blender. Liquify and pour into emp-ty Menu-ette. Cover with lid. Cook **3 minutes (_____) at 100% power.**
1/2 tsp. dried mint leaves	
1/8 tsp. coriander	
1/8 tsp. salt	
1/16 tsp. white pepper	
2 tbsp. heavy cream	Add cream and cover with lid. Cook **30 seconds (_____) at 100% pow-er.** Stir, pour into soup bowl, and serve.

SHRIMP SOUP

4 oz. fresh shrimp or 3 oz. frozen shrimp or langostinos

Shell, devein, and wash fresh shrimp. Do not defrost frozen shrimp. Chop shrimp into fine pieces.

1 tsp. butter

Put butter into 1½-quart Corning Ware pot. Cook **30 seconds (_____) at 100% power.** Add shrimp. Cook **30 seconds (_____) at 100% power** for fresh shrimp, **1 minute (_____) at 100% power** for frozen shrimp. Remove shrimp with slotted spoon and place in custard cup.

2 tsp. minced fresh or frozen onion
1/3 cup heavy cream*
1/3 cup milk*
1½ tsp. sherry
dash of white pepper
dash of salt
1 tsp. cornstarch

Put onion into pot. Cook **30 seconds (_____) at 100% power.** Add remaining ingredients to pot. Mix with wire whisk. Cook **3 minutes (_____) at 100% power,** stirring soup halfway through cooking time. Add shrimp to pot. Cover with lid. Cook **1 minute (_____) at 100% power.**

1 slice bread, toasted

Pour soup into bowl. Serve with toast.

* 2/3 cup half and half may be substituted for heavy cream and milk.

TOMATO SOUP

1 tsp. butter
1 oz. chopped fresh or
   frozen carrot
1 oz. minced celery
10-oz. tomato, chopped
1 tsp. fresh or frozen
   tomato paste
1/8 tsp. thyme
1/2 tsp. dried parsley or
   1½ tsp. minced fresh
   or frozen parsley
1/8 tsp. white pepper

Place butter, vegetables, and spices into 1½-pint Menu-ette. Cover with lid. Cook **10 minutes (_____) at 100% power.** Put into blender and liquify. Return to Menu-ette.

1/3 cup water

Pour water into empty blender. Turn blender on to absorb leftover tomato mixture and empty into Menu-ette. Cover with lid. Cook **1 minute (_____) at 100% power,** then cook **4 minutes (_____) at 50% power.**

2 tbsp. half and half

Add half and half. Mix well and cover with lid. Cook **30 seconds (_____) at 100% power.** Pour into soup bowl and serve.

VEGETABLE SOUP

1/4 slice fresh or frozen bacon, cut into 1/2-inch pieces

Place bacon in Gravy Maker Pot. Cook **1 minute (_____) at 100% power.**

2-oz. fresh or frozen lean ground beef pattie, 1/2-inch thick

Cut pattie into 1-inch squares and add to pot. Cook **1 minute (_____) at 100% power.**

2/3 cup water
1 beef bouillon cube
1 tbsp. all-purpose flour

Pour water into 1-cup liquid measure. Add bouillon cube and flour. Mix well and add to pot.

1 tbsp. chopped fresh or frozen onion
2 oz. tomato, cut into 1/2-inch cubes
1 tsp. fresh or frozen green pepper, cut into 1/2-inch cubes
1 tbsp. celery, cut into 1/4-inch cubes
1/3 cup fresh or frozen carrot, cut into 1/4-inch cubes
1/4 cup fresh or frozen whole-kernel corn*
1/2 tsp. dried parsley or 1½ tsp. minced fresh or frozen parsley
1/8 tsp. thyme
1/2-inch piece of bay leaf

Add remaining ingredients and cover with lid. Cook **7 minutes (_____) at 100% power.** Remove and discard bay leaf. Pour soup into bowl and serve.

* A medium-sized ear of corn will supply 1/4 cup. Use only the tender outside parts of the kernels.

POTATO VEGETABLE SOUP

2-oz. baking potato with skin or 2-oz. piece of baking potato

If potato is whole, puncture skin with fork. Wrap potato in paper towel. Cook **1:30 minutes (_____) at 100% power.** Set aside.

1/2 tsp. butter
2-oz. fresh or frozen lean ground beef pattie, 1/2-inch thick

Put butter into Gravy Maker Pot. Cut pattie into 1-inch squares and add to pot. Cook **1 minute (_____) at 100% power.** Stir. Cook **30 seconds (_____) at 100% power.**

2/3 cup water
1 beef bouillon cube
1 tbsp. all-purpose flour

Pour water into 1-cup liquid measure. Add bouillon cube. Cook **1:30 minutes (_____) at 100% power.** Add flour and mix well. Add to pot.

1/2 cup fresh or frozen mixed vegetables

Add vegetables to pot. Unwrap potato, peel skin, and cut into 1/2-inch cubes. Add to soup and cover with lid. Cook **7 minutes (_____) at 100% power.** Pour into soup bowl and serve.

GARDEN-FRESH VEGETABLE SOUP

2-oz. baking potato with skin or 2-oz. piece of baking potato

If potato is whole, puncture skin with fork. Wrap potato in paper towel. Cook **1:30 minutes (_____) at 100% power.** Set aside.

1 oz. mushrooms

Wash or brush mushrooms clean. Slice and spread on paper plate. Cover with paper towel. Cook **30 seconds (_____) at 100% power.** Set aside.

1/4 tsp. olive or vegetable oil
2 oz. fresh or frozen lean ground beef pattie, 1/2-inch thick

Put oil into Gravy Maker Pot. Cut pattie into 1-inch squares and add to pot. Cook **1 minute (_____) at 100% power.**

2/3 cup water
1 beef bouillon cube
1 tbsp. all-purpose flour

Put water, bouillon cube, and flour into 1-cup liquid measure. Mix well and add to pot. Unwrap potato, peel and cut into 1/2-inch cubes. Add to pot.

1 tbsp. chopped fresh or frozen onion
1 tbsp. chopped celery
piece of celery leaf
2 oz. tomato, chopped fine
1 tbsp. chopped fresh or frozen carrot
dash of garlic powder
1/8 tsp. marjoram
1/2-inch piece of bay leaf

Add remaining ingredients to pot. Cover with lid. Cook **7 minutes (_____) at 100% power.** Remove and discard bay leaf. Pour into soup bowl and serve.

SANDWICHES

CHICKEN SALAD SANDWICH

**7-oz. chicken breast or
thigh, skinned
1/4 tsp. salt
1/4 tsp. pepper
1 tbsp. dry white wine
(optional)**

Wash chicken and pat dry with paper towel. Sprinkle with salt and pepper. Place in Menu-ette Skillet, add wine and cover with lid. Cook **3:25 minutes (_____) at 100% power.** Pull meat from bone with fork and cut into bite-size pieces. Place in small bowl.

**1 tbsp. chopped celery or
water chestnut
2 tbsp. mayonnaise**

Add celery and mayonnaise to chicken. Mix well. Chill in refrigerator **30 minutes (_____).**

**2 slices bread
1 lettuce leaf (optional)**

Spread chicken salad on one slice of bread. Cover with lettuce and other slice of bread. Cut sandwich in half and serve.

EGG SALAD SANDWICH

butter
1 extra-large egg or
  2 small eggs
1/4 tsp. water

Butter custard cup. Break egg into cup. Puncture egg yolk with fork, then sprinkle with water. Cover cup with Menuette glass lid. Cook **30 seconds** (_____) **at 100% power.** Turn cup halfway around. Cook **25 seconds** (_____) **at 100% power** until egg is hardcooked. (Autorotating oven: Eliminate turn.) Chill in refrigerator **20 minutes** (_____).

1 tsp. mayonnaise
1/2 tsp. minced fresh or
  frozen onion
2 slices bread
1 lettuce leaf (optional)

Mash egg in cup with fork. Add mayonnaise and onion. Mix well. Spread on one slice of bread. Cover with lettuce leaf and other slice of bread. Cut sandwich in half and serve.

FRIED EGG SANDWICH

1 tsp. butter

Heat 6″ browning skillet **2 minutes** (_____) **at 100% power.** Place skillet on counter and run butter around bottom to coat generously.

1 extra-large egg
pinch of salt (optional)

Break egg into skillet. Sprinkle salt on egg yolk. Cover skillet with lid. Cook **50 seconds** (_____) **at 100% power.** Turn egg over with slotted turner. Cook **10 seconds** (_____) **at 100% power.**

2 slices bread

Use turner to place egg on one slice of bread. Break egg yolk over egg white with knife. Soak up remaining butter in skillet with other slice of bread and place on top of egg, buttered side down. Cut sandwich in half and serve.

GRILLED CHEESE SANDWICH

2 slices bread or 1 sliced English muffin

Toast bread in toaster. Place on paper plate with bottom edges touching.

1½ oz. cheese (American, Swiss, cheddar, etc.)*

Cover each slice of bread with a slice of cheese. Cook **20 seconds (_____) at 100% power** until cheese is bubbly. Put slices of toast together with cheese in between. Let cool **2 minutes (_____)**. Cut sandwich in half and serve.

* Use more than 1½ oz. cheese if needed to cover larger bread slices. Increase cooking time to **30 seconds (_____) at 100% power.**

Variation: After cheese is melted, place cooked bacon, slices of tomato, or pickles on top of cheese on one slice of bread. Cover with second slice of bread.

VEGETARIAN DELIGHT SANDWICH

1½ oz. thinly sliced onion

Spread onion evenly on paper plate and cover with paper towel. Cook **1 minute (_____) at 100% power.**

2 slices bread
1½ slices American cheese
2 oz. sliced tomato
1 oz. green pepper, sliced paper-thin

Place one slice of bread on paper plate and top with cooked onions, cheese, tomato, green pepper and other slice of bread. Cook **1 minute (_____) at 100% power** until cheese melts. Let cool **2 minutes (_____)**. Cut sandwich in half and serve.

HAM AND CHEESE SANDWICH

2 slices rye bread
3 slices American cheese

Place bread on paper plate with bottom edges touching. Lay 1½ cheese slices on each slice of bread.

1½ oz. cooked ham

Place ham on top of cheese on one slice of bread. If using leftover Ham Slice (see recipe), slice ham 1/8-inch thick before placing on cheese. Cook **40 seconds (_____) at 100% power** until cheese melts. Cover with other slice of bread and cheese. Cut sandwich in half with serrated knife and serve.

PATTIE MELT

2 slices rye bread

Toast bread and set aside.

4 oz. lean ground beef

Heat 6″ browning skillet **2 minutes (_____) at 100% power.** Form beef into pattie the same size and shape as the bread. Place pattie in skillet. Cover skillet with paper towel. Cook **45 seconds (_____) at 100% power.**

1/8 tsp. black pepper
1½ oz. Swiss cheese
 (1 slice, cut in half)

Turn pattie over and sprinkle with pepper. Cook **30 seconds (_____) at 100% power.** Place one slice of toast on paper plate. Lay one half of cheese slice on slice of toast and top with pattie, remaining cheese, and other slice of toast. Cook **25 seconds (_____) at 100% power** until cheese melts. Cut sandwich in half and serve.

SLOPPY JOE SANDWICH

3 oz. lean ground beef*
1 tbsp. chopped fresh or
frozen onion
1 tbsp. ketchup
1/2 tsp. mustard
1/8 tsp. chili powder
1/2 tsp. Worcestershire
sauce
1/8 tsp. salt
dash of black pepper

Place beef in 1½-pint Menu-ette. Break up beef with fork. Cook **1 minute** (_____) **at 100% power.** Beef will still be pink; mix well with fork until pink color is gone. Add onion, condiments, and spices to Menu-ette. Mix well with rubber spatula. Cover Menu-ette with paper towel. Cook **1 minute** (_____) **at 100% power.** Set aside.

1 unsliced hamburger roll

Slice off top portion of roll and set aside. Press down inside of roll with a small spoon to form a hollow. Fill hollow with meat filling and cover with sliced-off crust.

* Unless top-quality ground beef is used, grease will ooze out of meat filling into roll. Pour off grease or absorb it with paper towel before putting filling into roll.

BARBECUE BEEF SANDWICH

3 oz. cooked beef or pork
roast, sliced very thin

Place meat on paper plate. Cover with paper towel. Cook **25 seconds** (_____) **at 100% power** until meat is heated through.

2 slices bread or 1 sliced
hamburger roll
1 tbsp. barbecue sauce

Lay bread or roll open on plate. Spread sauce on each slice of bread. Place heated meat on sauce side of one slice of bread. Cover with sauce side of other slice. Cut sandwich in half and serve.

STEAK SANDWICH

1 tsp. butter

Put butter into small paper cup or custard cup. Cook **20 seconds (_____) at 100% power** to soften.

4 oz. beef, sliced paper-thin (sandwich or breakfast steaks)

If beef is not paper-thin, flatten with meat pounder. Place beef slices on paper plate. Spread or brush butter on one side of each slice. Set aside.

Heat browning grill **2:30 minutes** (_____) **at 100% power.** Place beef slices on grill, buttered side down. Cook **30 seconds (_____) at 100% power.**

1/8 tsp. salt
1/8 tsp. black pepper

Turn beef over with finger tongs and sprinkle with salt and pepper. Cook **15 seconds (_____) at 100% power.**

1 sliced hamburger roll or hard-crusted roll

Place beef on bottom half of roll. Rub top half of roll across grill to absorb drippings and place on top of beef. Serve.

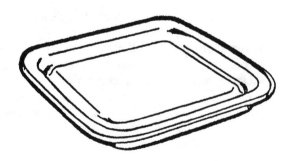

REUBEN SANDWICH

4 oz. sauerkraut
1/2 cup water

Put sauerkraut and water into 1½-pint Menu-ette. Cover with lid. Cook **2 minutes (_____) at 100% power.** Pour sauerkraut into strainer and set aside to drain.

3-4 oz. sliced corned beef
or pastrami*

Place meat on paper plate. Cover with paper towel. Cook **45 seconds (_____) at 100% power** until meat is hot.

2 slices rye bread
1/2 tsp. mustard
3/4 oz. Swiss cheese

Place one slice of bread on paper plate. Top with sauerkraut, meat, mustard, cheese, and other slice of bread. Cover with paper towel. Cook **45 seconds (_____) at 100% power** until cheese melts. Cut sandwich in half and serve.

* Packaged corned beef and pastrami are vacuum packed, so they keep well in the refrigerator for a long time. You may find these more practical to keep on hand. However, the freshly sliced corned beef and pastrami sold in delicatessens cook just as well in this recipe.

HOT DOG

2-oz. frankfurter
1 hot dog roll

Put frankfurter in roll and place on corner of paper towel. Fold towel deli-style: fold corner of towel over roll, then fold 2 side corners over the roll and wrap rest of towel around roll. Cook **45 seconds (_____) at 100% power.** (If frankfurter and roll are frozen, cook **50 seconds (_____) at 100% power.**)

mustard, ketchup, relish

Unwrap hot dog and garnish with desired condiments. Do not add condiments before cooking; they may burn.

Variation: Hot Dog and Sauerkraut

2 oz. sauerkraut

Put sauerkraut into strainer and rinse under faucet. Place in 1-pint Menu-ette and cover with lid. Cook **1 minute (_____) at 100% power.** Set aside.

2-oz. frankfurter
1 hot dog roll
mustard

Cook frankfurter in roll following basic recipe above. Garnish hot dog with sauerkraut and mustard.

CHEESE HOT DOG

2-oz. frankfurter
1/2 slice American cheese

Cut slit in frankfurter lengthwise. Do not cut all the way through. Fold cheese in half lengthwise and insert into slit in frankfurter.

1 hot dog roll
mustard, ketchup, relish

Lay frankfurter in roll, cheese side down. Wrap roll in paper towel deli-style (see Hot Dog recipe). Cook **45 seconds (_____) at 100% power.** Garnish with condiments after cooking.

HAMBURGER

4 oz. lean ground beef

Shape beef into 5-inch pattie on paper towel and set aside. Heat 6" browning skillet **2 minutes (_____) at 100% power.** Place pattie in skillet and cover with paper towel. Cook **35 seconds (_____) at 100% power.**

1/16 tsp. salt
1/8 tsp. black pepper

Discard paper towel. Turn pattie over and sprinkle with salt and pepper. Cook **35 seconds (_____) at 100% power.** Serve as is or on hamburger roll.

CORIANDER HAMBURGER

4 oz. lean ground beef
1 tbsp. beaten egg
1/4 tsp. ground coriander*
1/8 tsp. salt
1/16 tsp. cumin
1/16 tsp. black pepper
1/16 tsp. minced fresh or
  frozen garlic
pinch of nutmeg

Mix all ingredients in 1-quart mixing bowl. Shape into 4½-inch pattie and set aside. Heat 6" browning skillet **2:15 minutes (_____) at 100% power.** Place pattie in skillet and cover with paper towel. Cook **1 minute (_____) at 100% power.** Turn pattie over. Cook **45 seconds(_____) at 100% power.** Let stand **1 minute (_____).** Place on plate and serve.

* If only whole coriander is available, grind in mortar and pestle.

ONION HAMBURGER

3 oz. lean ground beef
1 tsp. dry bread crumbs
1 tsp. minced fresh or
   frozen onion
1/8 tsp. salt
1/4 tsp. Worcestershire sauce
dash of black pepper
1 tbsp. milk

Mix all ingredients in 1-quart mixing bowl. Shape into 5-inch pattie and set aside. Heat 6″ browning skillet **2 minutes** (_____) **at 100% power.** Place pattie in skillet and cover skillet with paper towel. Cook **1:30 minutes at 100% power,** turning pattie over halfway through cooking time. Let stand **1 minute** (_____). Place on plate and serve.

PARMESAN BURGER

3 oz. lean ground beef
2 tsp. grated Parmesan
   cheese
2 tsp. minced green onion
1 tsp. dried parsley or
   4 tsp. minced fresh or
   frozen parsley
1 tbsp. beaten egg
1/2 tsp. water
dash of salt
dash of cayenne pepper

Mix all ingredients in 1-quart mixing bowl. Shape into 4½-inch pattie and set aside. Heat 6″ browning skillet **2:15 minutes** (_____) **at 100% power.** Place pattie in skillet and cover skillet with paper towel. Cook **1 minute** (_____) **at 100% power.** Turn pattie over. Cook **45 seconds** (_____) **at 100% power.** Let stand **1 minute** (_____). Place on plate and serve.

CHEF'S HAMBURGER

3/4-oz. slice bread
1/4 cup water

Soak bread in water and set aside.

4 oz. lean ground beef
2 tbsp. minced fresh or
frozen onion
1/8 tsp. minced fresh or
frozen garlic
pinch of salt
pinch of black pepper
dash of Worcestershire sauce
1/2 tsp. dried basil

Mix ground beef, onion, garlic, and spices in 1-quart mixing bowl. Squeeze water out of bread and add bread to mixture. Shape into 4½-inch pattie. Place in Menu-ette Skillet.

1/2 tsp. Kitchen Bouquet

Spread Kitchen Bouquet evenly over pattie with back of measuring spoon. Cook **1:30 minutes (_____) at 100% power.** Turn skillet halfway around. Cook **1 minute (_____) at 100% power.** (Autorotating oven: Eliminate turn.) Let stand **1 minute (_____).** Place on plate and serve.

MUSHROOM HAMBURGER

1/2 oz. mushrooms
1 tbsp. minced fresh or
   frozen onion

Wash or brush mushrooms clean. Chop and spread on paper plate. Add onion and cover with paper towel. Cook **1 minute (_____) at 100% power.** Set aside to cool.

4 oz. lean ground beef
1/8 tsp. salt
1/4 tsp. black pepper

Mix ground beef, onions, and mushrooms in 1-quart mixing bowl. Shape into 5-inch pattie and set aside. Heat 6" browning skillet **2 minutes (_____) at 100% power.** Place pattie in skillet. Cook **45 seconds (_____) at 100% power.** Turn pattie over and sprinkle with salt and pepper. Cook **45 seconds (_____) at 100% power.** Let stand **1 minute (_____).** Place on plate and serve.

CHILI HAMBURGER

4 oz. lean ground beef
1 tbsp. bottled chili sauce
1/2 tsp. mustard
1/4 tsp. horseradish
1/4 tsp. minced fresh or
   frozen onion
1/4 tsp. Worcestershire
   sauce
1/8 tsp. salt
hamburger roll (optional)

Mix all ingredients in 1-quart mixing bowl. Shape into 4½-inch pattie and set aside. Heat 6" browning skillet **2 minutes (_____) at 100% power.** Place pattie in skillet. Cook **45 seconds (_____) at 100% power.** Turn pattie over. Cook **30 seconds (_____) at 100% power.** Let stand **1 minute (_____).** Serve as is or on hamburger roll.

CHEESEBURGER

4 oz. lean ground beef
1/4 tsp. black pepper

Shape beef into 5-inch pattie on paper towel and set aside. Heat 6″ browning skillet **2 minutes (_____) at 100% power.** Place pattie in skillet and cover skillet with paper towel. Cook **35 seconds (_____) at 100% power.** Turn pattie over and sprinkle with pepper. Replace paper towel. Cook **15 seconds (_____) at 100% power.**

1 slice American cheese
hamburger roll (optional)

Discard paper towel. Place cheese on top of pattie. Cook **20 seconds (_____) at 100% power** until cheese melts. Serve as is or on hamburger roll.

BACON CHEESEBURGER

2 slices bacon

Place paper towel on paper plate. Place bacon on paper towel and cover with another paper towel. Cook **1:45 minutes** (_____) **at 100% power** until bacon is crisp. Set aside.

1 sliced hamburger roll

Press each half of hamburger roll flat with palm of hand so halves will fit into toaster. Toast lightly. Place roll open on plate and set aside.

4 oz. lean ground beef
1/4 tsp. black pepper

Shape ground beef into 5-inch pattie on paper towel and set aside. Heat 6″ browning skillet **2 minutes** (_____) **at 100% power.** Put pattie in skillet and cover skillet with paper towel. Cook **35 seconds** (_____) **at 100% power.** Discard paper towel. Turn pattie over and sprinkle with pepper. Cook **15 seconds** (_____) **at 100% power.**

1 slice American cheese
1 large or 2 small tomato slices

Top pattie with cheese. Cook **20 seconds** (_____) **at 100% power** until cheese is melted and bubbly. Place pattie on bottom half of roll. Fold bacon slice in half and place on top of cheese. Cover bacon with tomato and top of roll and serve.

LITTLE PIZZAS

1 English muffin, halved

Toast muffin lightly and set aside.

1/2 tsp. olive oil
1 tiny peeled garlic clove

Place oil and garlic in 1/2-cup ceramic measuring cup with handle. Set cup on its side in oven so that oil covers garlic but does not spill. Cook **1 minute** (_____) **at 100% power.** Discard garlic.

3 tbsp. (3 oz.) tomato sauce
1/4 tsp. oregano

Add tomato sauce and oregano to cup. Cover with Menu-ette lid. Cook **2 minutes** (_____) **at 100% power.** Place muffin on paper plate, cut sides up. Spread sauce on each half.

1 oz. Mozzarella cheese

Grate cheese or cut into 3 slices 1/8-inch thick. Distribute cheese evenly over sauce. Cook **40 seconds** (_____) **at 100% power** until cheese melts. Let stand **2 minutes** (_____) until cheese cools and serve.

EGG, PASTA, AND RICE DISHES

CHEESE 'N' EGG

1/2 tsp. butter
1 slice white bread
2 oz. Swiss cheese

Spread butter on bread and place in Petite Pan. Bread will be too large; push down until it fits in pan. Cut cheese into 1-inch squares. Sprinkle over bread.

1 small egg
1/4 cup half and half
1/8 tsp. salt
dash of paprika
dash of cayenne pepper
1/8 tsp. dry mustard

Put remaining ingredients into small bowl and beat with wire whisk. Pour mixture over cheese in pan. Cook **2 minutes** (_____) **at 100% power,** rotating pan a quarter-turn every **30 seconds** (_____). (Autorotating oven: Eliminate turns.) Let stand **4 minutes** (_____) and serve.

MOMMA'S EGG DIABLE

1/2 tsp. olive oil
1 tiny peeled garlic clove

Place oil and garlic in 1/2-cup ceramic measuring cup with handle. Set cup on its side in oven so that oil covers garlic but does not spill. Cook **1 minute (_____) at 100% power.** Discard garlic.

3 tbsp. (3 oz.) tomato
   sauce
1/4 tsp. oregano

Add tomato sauce and oregano to cup. Cook **1 minute (_____) at 100% power.** Stir.

1 extra-large egg

Add egg to sauce. Carefully puncture yolk with fork. Cover cup with Menuette lid. Cook **1 minute (_____) at 100% power** until egg white is cooked. Hold cup by handle, scoop out contents into small cereal bowl and serve.

EGG FLORENTINE

1 cup frozen spinach or 4 oz. washed fresh spinach*
1/4 tsp. salt

Place spinach in 1½-pint Menu-ette. Cover with lid. Cook **3 minutes** (_____) **at 100% power.** Sprinkle spinach with salt, mix with fork, and drain in small strainer. Press out excess water with rubber spatula. Put spinach into 1-cup ceramic measuring cup with handle, patting spinach down in cup bottom and forming a 1-inch ridge around the inside like a pie crust.

1 extra-large egg or 2 small eggs
dash of black pepper
1 tbsp. heavy cream
2 tsp. grated Romano or Parmesan cheese

Break egg into center of spinach. Puncture yolk with fork. Sprinkle egg with pepper. Slowly pour cream on top of egg. Cover cream with cheese. Cook **2 minutes** (_____) **at 100% power.** Serve egg in cup or transfer egg to small dish.

* To obtain 4 oz. washed fresh spinach, start with about 6 oz. fresh spinach. Remove the bad leaves and the tough stems. Place spinach in sink and fill with water. Swish water around to dislodge sand, then allow sand to settle at bottom, leaving spinach floating. Scoop up spinach with your hards or a strainer.

ASPARAGUS OMELET

Note: In this recipe and those that follow, the omelets are cooked in a mixing bowl for convenience. For a browned omelet, heat 6" browning skillet for **1 minute (_____) at 100% power,** pour in contents of mixing bowl, and cook **1 minute (_____) at 100% power** until omelet sets. Place omelet on plate with slotted turner and serve.

1½ oz. frozen asparagus spears (3 spears)

Separate asparagus with blunt knife. Place in Menu-ette Skillet and cover with lid. Cook **1:30 minutes (_____) at 100% power.** Cut into 1-inch pieces and set aside.

1 extra-large egg or
  2 small eggs
1 tbsp. milk
1/8 tsp. salt
1/16 tsp. black pepper
1/4 tsp. dried chopped chives
1/4 tsp. dried parsley or
  3/4 tsp. minced fresh or
  frozen parsley

Put egg, milk, and seasonings into 1-quart mixing bowl and beat well with wire whisk.

1 tsp. butter (optional)

Add butter and cooked asparagus to mixture and stir. Cook **1:20 minutes (_____) at 100% power** until 1 tbsp. egg remains uncooked. Mix with rubber spatula and serve.

ASPARAGUS AND HAM OMELET

1 oz. frozen asparagus spears (2 spears)

Separate asparagus with blunt knife. Place in Menu-ette Skillet and cover with lid. Cook **1 minute (_____) at 100% power.** Cut asparagus into 1-inch pieces and set aside.

**1 extra-large egg or
2 small eggs
1 tbsp. milk
1/16 tsp. salt
1/16 tsp. black pepper**

Put egg, milk, salt, and pepper into 1-quart mixing bowl. Beat well with wire whisk.

**1 tbsp. (1/2 oz.) chopped cooked ham
1 tsp. butter (optional)**

Add ham, butter, and asparagus to egg mixture. Stir. Cook **1:15 minutes (_____) at 100% power** until 1 tbsp. egg remains uncooked. Mix with rubber spatula and serve. (See recipe for Asparagus Omelet for instructions on preparing omelet in browning skillet.)

MOZZARELLA CHEESE OMELET

**1 extra-large egg or
2 small eggs
1 tbsp. milk
1/16 tsp. salt
1/16 tsp. black pepper
1 tsp. butter (optional)**

Place egg, milk, salt, and pepper in Menu-ette Skillet. Beat well with wire whisk. Add butter. Cook **40 seconds (_____) at 100% power.**

1 oz. grated Mozzarella cheese

Sprinkle cheese over egg. Cook **40 seconds (_____) at 100% power** until cheese melts. Serve. (See recipe for Asparagus Omelet for instructions on preparing omelet in browning skillet.)

GREEN PEPPER OMELET

2 oz. green pepper

Cut green pepper into 1-inch squares. Spread evenly on paper plate and cover with paper towel. Cook **1:20 minutes** (_____) **at 100% power.** Set aside.

**1 extra-large egg or
 2 small eggs
1 tbsp. milk
1/8 tsp. salt
1/8 tsp. black pepper
1 tsp. butter (optional)**

Put egg, milk, salt, and pepper into 1-quart mixing bowl and beat well with wire whisk. Add butter and cooked green pepper. Mix with rubber spatula. Cook **1:25 minutes** (_____) **at 100% power** until 1 tbsp. egg remains uncooked. Mix with rubber spatula and serve. (See recipe for Asparagus Omelet for instructions on preparing omelet in browning skillet.)

Variation: Pepper and Onion Omelet—decrease green pepper to 1 oz. and add 1 oz. sliced onion.

MUSHROOM OMELET

1 oz. mushrooms

Brush or wash mushrooms clean and drain on paper towel. Slice and spread evenly on paper plate. Cover with paper towel. Cook **30 seconds** (_____) **at 100% power.** Set aside.

**1 extra-large egg or
 2 small eggs
1 tbsp. milk
1/8 tsp. salt
pinch of black pepper
1 tsp. butter (optional)**

Put egg, milk, salt, and pepper into 1-quart mixing bowl and beat well with wire whisk. Add butter and cooked mushrooms. Mix with rubber spatula. Cook **1:25 minutes** (_____) **at 100% power** until 1 tbsp. egg remains uncooked. Mix with rubber spatula and serve. (See Asparagus Omelet recipe for instructions on preparing omelet in browning skillet.)

ONION OMELET

2½-oz. onion

Peel and slice onion. Spread out evenly on paper plate and cover with paper towel. Cook **1:20 minutes** (_____) **at 100% power** until tip of at least one onion slice turns brown.

1 extra-large egg or
2 small eggs
1 tbsp. milk
1/8 tsp. salt
1/8 tsp. black pepper
1 tsp. butter (optional)

Put egg, milk, salt, and pepper into 1-quart mixing bowl and beat well with wire whisk. Add butter and cooked onions. Cook **1:25 minutes** (_____) **at 100% power** until 1 tbsp. egg remains uncooked. Mix with rubber spatula and serve. (See Asparagus Omelet recipe for instructions on preparing omelet in browning skillet.)

SHRIMP OMELET

2 oz. fresh shrimp in shells*
1/4 tsp. Old Bay Seasoning or other Chesapeake Bay-style seasoning
1/16 tsp. salt

Wash shrimp and place on paper plate. Sprinkle with Old Bay Seasoning and salt. Cover with paper towel. Cook **45 seconds (_____) at 100% power.** Set aside to cool.

1 extra-large egg or 2 small eggs
1 tbsp. milk
1/8 tsp. salt
1/8 tsp. pepper

Put egg, milk, salt, and pepper into 1-quart mixing bowl and beat well with wire whisk. Set aside.

1 tsp. butter (optional)

Peel and devein shrimp and cut into 1/2-inch pieces. Add shrimp and butter to egg mixture and mix with rubber spatula. Cook **1:20 minutes (_____) at 100% power** until 1 tbsp. egg remains uncooked. Mix with rubber spatula and serve. (See Asparagus Omelet recipe for instructions on preparing omelet in browning skillet.)

* 1 oz. frozen cooked shrimp, defrosted, may be substituted in third step.

EGG NOODLES

Note: To double or triple this recipe, cook noodles **6 minutes (＿＿＿)** **at 50% power.**

1½ cups water

Pour water into 1½-quart Corning Ware pot. Cook **3:45 minutes (＿＿＿)** **at 100% power** until water boils.

1/8 tsp. salt
1/8 tsp. vegetable oil or
butter
1 cup (2 oz.) egg noodles

Add salt and oil to water and stir. Add noodles and spread out evenly in pot. Cook **4 minutes (＿＿＿) at 100% power.** Stir and cover pot with lid. Let stand for at least **5 minutes (＿＿＿)** or until rest of meal is prepared.

1 tbsp. butter

Final preparation: Drain noodles and return to pot. Add butter. Cover pot with lid. Cook **1 minute (＿＿＿) at 100% power** or until noodles are hot. Serve.

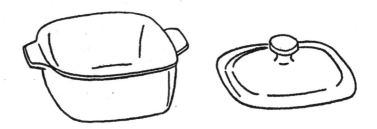

MACARONI

Method 1: To cook small macaroni (elbow, rotelle, ziti, etc.):

1 cup water
1/4 tsp. salt
1/4 tsp. vegetable oil

Pour water into 1½-quart Corning Ware pot. Cook **2:30 minutes** (_____) **at 100% power** until water boils. Add salt and oil to water and stir.

2 oz. macaroni

Spread out macaroni in pot. Cook **12 minutes** (_____) **at 50% power** until water is absorbed. Place on plate, top with your favorite sauce, and serve. (See recipes for Pasta Sauce and Vegetarian Pasta Sauce.)

Method 2: To cook long macaroni (linguine, spaghetti, vermicelli, etc.):

2 cups water
1/4 tsp. salt
1/4 tsp. vegetable oil

Pour water into 1½-quart Corning Ware pot. Cook **5 minutes** (_____) **at 100% power** until water boils. Add salt and oil to water and stir.

2 oz. macaroni

Place macaroni in pot. Ends will stick out of pot. Cook **1 minute** (_____) **at 100% power.** The macaroni in the water will have softened. Push exposed ends down into pot. Cook **1 minute** (_____) **at 100% power.** Stir macaroni with fork, making sure all of it is covered by water. Cook **6 minutes** (_____) **(8 minutes [_____] for spaghetti) at 50% power** until macaroni is done. Drain macaroni in strainer. Place on plate, top with your favorite sauce, and serve. (See recipes for Pasta Sauce and Vegetarian Pasta Sauce.)

Note: To increase this recipe, add 1 cup water for each additional 2 oz. of macaroni. Cook water until it boils, then follow recipe as given. Cooking time remains the same.

PASTINA

1 cup water

Pour water into 1½-pint Menu-ette. Cook **2:30 minutes** (_____) at **100% power** until water boils.

1/8 tsp. salt
1/3 cup (2 oz.) pastina
1 tbsp. butter

Add salt and pastina. Spread pastina evenly in Menu-ette. Cook **3 minutes** (_____) **at 100% power**. Add butter, stir, and serve.

MACARONI AND CHEESE

1 cup water

Pour water into 1½-quart Corning Ware pot. Cook **2:30 minutes** (_____) **at 100% power** until water boils.

1/4 tsp. salt
1/4 tsp. vegetable oil
   or butter
2 oz. elbow macaroni

Add salt and oil and stir. Add macaroni and spread evenly in pot. Cook **12 minutes** (_____) **at 50% power**. Drain in strainer and set aside.

1 tsp. butter

Put butter into 1½-pint Menu-ette. Cook **20 seconds** (_____) **at 100% power** until melted.

1 tsp. all-purpose flour
1/16 tsp. dry mustard
1/16 tsp. paprika
1/8 tsp. salt
dash of black pepper
1/3 cup milk

Add flour and spices and stir well. Add milk and stir with wire whisk. Cook **1 minute** (_____) **at 100% power**. Stir again. Cook **1 minute** (_____) **at 100% power**.

1 oz. grated cheddar cheese
dash of Worcestershire sauce
1 tbsp. minced fresh or
   frozen onion

Add cheese, Worcestershire sauce, and onion. Stir well. Add drained macaroni and stir. Cook **1:15 minutes** (_____) **at 100% power**. Stir well.

2 tsp. dry bread crumbs
1/2 oz. grated cheddar
   cheese
1/16 tsp. paprika

Sprinkle mixture with bread crumbs, then cheese, then paprika. Cook **1:15 minutes** (_____) **at 100% power**. Let stand **5 minutes** (_____). Serve in Menu-ette.

VERMICELLI AND EGGS

1 cup water

Pour water into 1½-quart Corning Ware pot. Cook **2:30 minutes (_____)** **at 100% power** until water boils.

1/4 tsp. salt
1/4 tsp. vegetable oil
2 oz. vermicelli

Add salt and oil to water and stir. Break vermicelli in half and spread evenly in water. Cook **12 minutes (_____) at** **50% power** or until water is absorbed. Fluff with fork and set aside.

1½ tbsp. olive oil
2 extra-large eggs or
  4 small eggs
1/4 tsp. salt

Pour oil into 8½" browning skillet. Cook **2 minutes (_____) at 100% pow-er.** Break eggs into skillet and sprinkle unbroken yolks with salt. Cover skillet with lid. Cook **1 minute (_____) at** **100% power.** (Eggs will be under-cooked.) Place vermicelli on top of eggs. Mix well with large fork and spoon until egg is evenly distributed throughout ver-micelli. Serve in skillet.

VERMICELLI WITH CLAM SAUCE

6 medium-sized clams*

Scrub clams with brush. Place in circle in 9" pie plate. Cook **2 minutes (_____) at 100% power** until all clams are open. Set aside to cool.

1 tsp. olive oil
1 small peeled garlic clove

Put oil and garlic in 1½-pint Menuette. Prop up one end with plastic jar lid so that oil will collect in one corner and cover garlic. Cook **2 minutes (_____) at 100% power.**

1 8-oz. can tomato sauce
1 tsp. oregano

Discard garlic. Remove prop so Menuette lies flat. Add tomato sauce and oregano and cover with lid. Cook **4 minutes (_____) at 100% power.** Meanwhile, cut through each clam muscle with sharp knife to open shells. Cut out clams and cut into 1/2-inch pieces. Add to sauce. Strain juice still in pie plate and add 2 tbsp. juice to sauce. Cook **1 minute (_____) at 100% power.** Set aside. Cook 2 oz. vermicelli (see recipe) and drain. Place on plate, cover with sauce, and serve.

* 1 6½-oz. can chopped clams may be substituted. To remove metallic taste, empty clams into strainer and wash thoroughly with cold water or white wine. Discard liquid and add clams to sauce.

NOODLE BAKE

1 cup water
1/8 tsp. salt
1½ oz. egg noodles

Pour water into 1-quart Corning Ware pot. Cook **2:30 minutes** (_____) **at 100% power** until water boils. Add salt and noodles. Cook **2 minutes** (_____) **at 50% power.** Set aside.

4 oz. lean ground beef
1/2 tbsp. butter
3 tbsp. (3 oz.) tomato sauce
1/8 tsp. salt
dash of black pepper
1/8 tsp. garlic salt

Put ground beef and butter into Gravy Maker Pot. Cook **2 minutes** (_____) **at 100% power.** Break up beef into small chunks with fork. Add tomato sauce and spices and mix well. Cook **20 seconds** (_____) **at 100% power** until mixture boils. Cook **1:15 minutes** (_____) **at 50% power.** Set aside. Drain noodles in strainer and set aside.

1/4 cup cottage cheese
1/4 cup sour cream
1 oz. chopped green onion
1/2 oz. grated cheddar
  cheese

Put cottage cheese, sour cream, and green onion into emptied pot and mix. In 1-pint Menu-ette, layer 1/3 of meat mixture, 1/2 of cheese mixture, and 1/2 of noodles. Repeat layers and put last 1/3 of meat mixture on top. Cover meat with cheddar cheese. Cook **2 minutes** (_____) **at 100% power,** giving Menu-ette a half-turn halfway through cooking time. (Autorotating oven: Eliminate turn.) Let stand **2 minutes** (_____). Serve in Menu-ette.

MACARONI BAKE

1/2 tsp. olive oil
3 oz. lean ground beef
1/8 tsp. minced fresh or
frozen garlic
3 tbsp. (3 oz.) tomato sauce
1/8 tsp. sugar
1/16 tsp. salt
1/16 tsp. black pepper

Place oil, ground beef, and garlic in Gravy Maker Pot. Cook **1:30 minutes (＿＿＿) at 100% power.** Break up beef with fork. Add tomato sauce, sugar, salt, and pepper. Cook **2 minutes (＿＿＿) at 50% power.** Set aside.

1 cup water
1/4 tsp. salt
1/4 tsp. vegetable oil
2 oz. elbow macaroni

Pour water into 1-quart Corning Ware pot. Cook **2:30 minutes (＿＿＿) at 100% power** until water boils. Add salt, oil, and macaroni. Spread macaroni evenly in pot. Cook **12 minutes (＿＿＿) at 50% power.** Drain in strainer and set aside.

2 tbsp. sour cream
1/2 oz. cream cheese
1 tsp. chopped green onion

Put sour cream, cream cheese, and green onion into emptied pot and mix well. Put cooked macaroni into 1½-pint Menu-ette. Spread cheese mixture on top, then meat mixture. Cook **2 minutes (＿＿＿) at 100% power.**

1 oz. grated cheddar cheese
or 1 slice of American
cheese, diced

Sprinkle cheddar cheese on top of macaroni. Cook **2 minutes (＿＿＿) at 100% power** until cheese melts. Let stand **2 minutes (＿＿＿).** Serve in Menu-ette.

MAFALDA (EASY LASAGNA)

1 cup water
1/8 tsp. salt
2 oz. mafalda* (8 noodles)

Pour water into 1½-quart Corning Ware pot. Cook **2:30 minutes** (_____) **at 100% power** until water boils. Add salt to pot. Break noodles in half and place in pot. Cook **2 minutes** (_____) **at 50% power**. Set aside.

4 oz. lean ground beef
4 oz. canned tomatoes or
   5 oz. chopped fresh
   tomatoes
1½ tbsp. unfrozen or
   frozen tomato paste
1/4 tsp. salt
1/4 tsp. dried basil
1/8 tsp. oregano
pinch of garlic powder
2 tbsp. water

Put ground beef in Gravy Maker Pot or Cook 'N' Pour Pan. Cook **30 seconds** (_____) **at 100% power**. Stir and break up ground beef into small pieces with fork. Cook **30 seconds** (_____) **at 100% power**. Add tomatoes, tomato paste, spices, and water. Cook **1:50 minutes** (_____) **at 100% power**. Set aside.

4 oz. (1/2 cup) ricotta
   cheese
1 tbsp. grated Parmesan
   cheese
2 tbsp. beaten egg
3/4 tsp. dried parsley or
   2½ tsp. minced fresh or
   frozen parsley

Mix cheeses, egg, and parsley in small bowl. Set aside.

2 oz. grated fresh or frozen
   Mozzarella cheese

Drain noodles in strainer and set aside. Put 6 tbsp. tomato mixture into emptied pot and spread evenly over bottom. Cover with half of noodles, then half of cheese mixture. Sprinkle half of Mozzarella cheese on top. Then repeat layering procedure with 1/4 cup sauce and the remaining noodles, cheese mixture, and Mozzarella cheese. Top with remaining sauce. Cover pot with plastic wrap. Cook **2 minutes** (_____) **at**

100% power. Give pot a quarter-turn. Cook **2 minutes (_____) at 100% power.** Give pot another quarter-turn. Cook **2:30 minutes (_____) at 50% power.** Give pot another quarter-turn. Cook **2:30 minutes (_____) at 50% power.** (Autorotating oven: Cook **4 minutes (_____) at 100% power,** then cook **5 minutes (_____) at 50% power.** Eliminate turns.)

1/2 tbsp. grated Romano cheese

Remove plastic wrap. Sprinkle cheese over all. Cook **30 seconds (_____) at 100% power.** Let stand for **10 minutes (_____) and serve.**

---

* Mafalda noodles look like lasagna noodles but are half as wide and are easier to break in half before cooking.

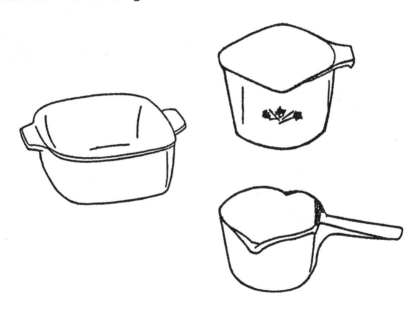

RAVIOLI

Pasta Sauce (see recipe)

Prepare sauce and set aside.

4 cups water
1 tsp. salt
1 tsp. vegetable oil

Pour water into 3-quart Corning Ware pot and cover with lid. Cook **10 minutes** (_____) **at 100% power** until water boils. Add salt and oil. Stir.

6 oz. frozen ravioli or homemade ravioli

Add ravioli one at a time. Cover pot with lid. Cook **4 minutes** (_____) **at 100% power,** then cook **16 minutes** (_____) **at 50% power.** Turn each ravioli over with slotted spoon and replace lid. Cook **4 minutes** (_____) **at 50% power.** Set aside.

Reheat Pasta Sauce **1 minute** (_____) **at 100% power.** Remove ravioli with slotted spoon and drain in strainer. Puncture each ravioli with fork to allow water to escape. Place ravioli on plate when completely drained.

2 tbsp. grated Romano cheese

Sprinkle with cheese and cover with sauce. Serve.

WHITE RICE

Note: Converted (parboiled) rice is a less sticky form of rice that is preferred for side dishes, salads, stews, and seafood dishes. Enriched long grain rice is a stickier form of rice that is good for puddings.

1 cup water

Pour water into 1-quart Corning Ware pot. Cook **2:30 minutes** (_____) **at 100% power** until water boils.

1/4 tsp. salt
1/4 tsp. butter
1/4 cup long grain or converted rice

Add salt, butter, and rice to water. Cover pot with lid. Cook **18 minutes** (_____) **at 30% power.** Set aside until rest of meal is prepared.

Final preparation: Drain rice in plastic strainer and put strainer into emptied pot. Cover with paper towel. Cook **1 minute** (_____) **at 100% power** until rice is dry and fluffy. Remove strainer, wipe out pot with paper towel, and put rice back into pot.

1 tsp. butter

Put butter in custard cup. Cook **20 seconds** (_____) **at 100% power** until melted. Pour over rice. (Butter can be melted directly on rice, but this extra step improves the taste.) Fluff with fork before serving.

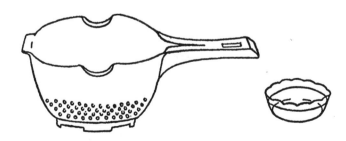

EGG, PASTA, AND RICE · 73

BROWN RICE

Note: Cooked brown rice is chewier and has a nutlike flavor. It is preferred for its higher nutritional value, but its oil content gives it a limited shelf life, unlike most rice.

1½ cups water
1/8 tsp. salt
1/4 tsp. butter
3 tbsp. long grain parboiled brown rice

Put water, salt, butter, and rice into 1-quart Corning Ware pot. Stir and cover pot with lid. Cook **14 minutes** (_____) **at 50% power.** Set aside until rest of meal is prepared.

Final preparation: Drain rice in plastic strainer and put strainer into emptied pot. Cover with paper towel. Cook **1 minute** (_____) **at 100% power** until rice is dry and fluffy. Remove strainer, wipe out pot with paper towel, and put rice back into pot.

2 tsp. butter

Put butter into custard cup. Cook **30 seconds** (_____) **at 100% power** until melted. Pour over rice. (Butter can be melted directly on rice, but this extra step improves the taste.) Fluff with fork before serving.

RICE AND CHEESE

1 tsp. butter
1/4 cup chopped fresh or
   frozen onion

Put butter and onion into 1-quart Corning Ware pot and cover with lid. Cook **2 minutes (_____) at 100% power.**

1/4 cup long grain or
   converted white rice
2/3 cup water
1/4 tsp. salt
1/16 tsp. black pepper

Add rice, water, salt, and pepper. Replace lid. Cook **2 minutes (_____) at 100% power,** then cook **21 minutes (_____) at 30% power** until water is completely absorbed.

1 oz. Swiss or Gruyere cheese
1/2 tsp. dried parsley or
  2 tsp. minced fresh or
   frozen parsley

Cut cheese into chunks. Add cheese and parsley to rice and mix with fork. Cover pot with lid. Set aside until rest of meal is prepared.

Final preparation: Cook **1 minute (_____) at 100% power** to heat before serving.

CURRIED RICE

1 tsp. butter
1 tbsp. chopped fresh or
   frozen onion

Put butter and onion into 1-quart Corning Ware pot. Cook **1 minute (_____) at 100% power.** Set aside.

2/3 cup water
1/2 chicken bouillon cube
1/4 cup long grain or
   converted white rice
1/8 tsp. mild curry powder
1/4 tsp. dried parsley or
  1 tsp. minced fresh or
   frozen parsley
dash of black pepper

Put water and bouillon cube into 1-cup liquid measure. Cook **1:30 minutes (_____) at 100% power.** Stir and add to mixture in pot. Add remaining ingredients and stir well. Cover pot with lid. Cook **18 minutes (_____) at 30% power.** Set aside until rest of meal is prepared.

Final preparation: Fluff rice with fork. Cook **1 minute (_____) at 100% power** to heat before serving.

RICE WITH DILL

1/4 tsp. butter
1 tbsp. chopped fresh
  or frozen onion

Put butter and onion into 1-quart Corning Ware pot. Cook **1 minute** (_____) **at 100% power.**

1/4 cup converted white rice
2/3 cup water
1/4 tsp. salt
pinch of black pepper
1/4 tsp. dill weed
1-inch piece of bay leaf
2 drops Tabasco sauce

Add remaining ingredients and cover pot with lid. Cook **2 minutes** (_____) **at 100% power,** then cook **18 minutes** (_____) **at 30% power.** Set aside until rest of meal is prepared.

Final preparation: Remove and discard bay leaf. Fluff rice with fork. Cook **1 minute** (_____) **at 100% power** to heat before serving.

DARK RICE

Note: This is a flavorful, dry rice.

1 tsp. butter
1 oz. chopped green onion
1 oz. chopped mushrooms

Place butter, onion, and mushrooms in 1½-pint Menu-ette. Cook **2 minutes** (_____) **at 100% power.**

2 tbsp. long grain or
converted white rice

Add rice. Cook **1:30 minutes** (_____) **at 100% power.** (Rice will look burned.) Set aside.

3/4 cup water
1/2 beef bouillon cube

Put water and bouillon cube into 1-cup liquid measure. Cook **2 minutes** (_____) **at 100% power** until mixture boils. Stir until bouillon cube dissolves. Add mixture to Menu-ette. Cover Menu-ette with lid. Cook **24 minutes** (_____) **at 30% power.** Drain rice in a strainer. Set strainer aside, wipe Menu-ette clean with paper towel, and put rice back into Menu-ette. Cover Menu-ette with lid. Let stand until rest of meal is prepared.

Final preparation: Cook rice **30 seconds** (_____) **at 100% power** to heat before serving.

RICE VERDE

3/4 cup water

Pour water into 1-quart Corning Ware pot. Cook **2:15 minutes (_____) at 100% power** until water boils.

1/4 tsp. salt
1/2 tsp. butter
1/4 cup long grain or converted white rice

Add salt and butter. Stir. Add rice and spread out evenly in pot. Cover pot with lid. Cook **18 minutes (_____) at 30% power.**

1 tsp. butter
2 tsp. chopped fresh or frozen onion

Put butter and onion into 1½-pint Menu-ette. Cook **1 minute (_____) at 100% power.** Drain rice in strainer and add to onion mixture.

1/2 tsp. dried parsley or 1 tsp. minced fresh or frozen parsley
pinch of thyme
dash of black pepper

Add parsley and spices to mixture and toss with fork to mix. Cover Menu-ette with lid. Cook **1 minute (_____) at 100% power.** Let stand until rest of meal is prepared.

Final preparation: Fluff rice with fork. Cook **1 minute (_____) at 100% power** to heat before serving.

MEXICAN RICE

1 tsp. olive oil
1/8 tsp. minced fresh or
  frozen garlic
2 tbsp. chopped green onion
1 tbsp. chopped fresh or
  frozen green pepper

Put oil, garlic, onion, and green pepper into 1-quart Corning Ware pot. Cook **1 minute (_____) at 100% power.** Set aside.

2/3 cup water
1/2 chicken bouillon cube
1/4 cup long grain or
  converted white rice
dash of salt
1/4 tsp. chili powder

Put water and bouillon cube into 1-cup liquid measure. Cook **1:30 minutes (_____) at 100% power.** Stir and add to pot. Add remaining ingredients and stir well. Cover pot with lid. Cook **18 minutes (_____) at 30% power.** Set aside until rest of meal is prepared.

Final preparation: Fluff rice with fork. Cook **1 minute (_____) at 100% power** to heat before serving.

RICE WITH MUSHROOMS

1/4 tsp. butter
2 tsp. chopped fresh or
  frozen onion

Put butter and onion into 1-quart Corning Ware pot. Cook **1 minute (_____) at 100% power.**

1/4 cup converted white rice
1 oz. chopped mushrooms
2/3 cup water
1/4 tsp. salt
dash of black pepper
1/2 tsp. dried parsley or
  1 tsp. minced fresh or
  frozen parsley

Add remaining ingredients and cover pot with lid. Cook **2 minutes (_____) at 100% power,** then cook **18 minutes (_____) at 30% power.** Set aside, covered, until rest of meal is prepared.

Final preparation: Fluff rice with fork. Cook **1 minute (_____) at 100% power** to heat before serving.

EGG-FRIED RICE

1/2 cup water

Pour water into Menu-ette Skillet. Cook **1:30 minutes (_____) at 100% power** until water boils.

1/8 tsp. salt
1/4 tsp. vegetable oil
2½ tbsp. converted white rice

Add salt, oil, and rice and spread evenly in skillet. Cover skillet with lid. Cook **10 minutes (_____) at 50% pow-er.** Pour rice into strainer and set aside.

1 small egg

Wipe skillet dry with paper towel. Put egg into skillet and beat with small wire whisk. Cook **55 seconds (_____) at 100% power** until egg is firm. Scrape egg out of skillet with rubber spatula and place on cutting board to cool.

1 tsp. vegetable oil
2 tbsp. (1 oz.) chopped fresh or frozen onion
3 tbsp. (1 oz.) chopped celery
1/8 tsp. minced fresh or frozen garlic

Put oil, onion, celery, and garlic into emptied skillet. Cook **2 minutes (_____) at 100% power.**

1/4 cup (1½ oz.) cooked pork*

Slice pork into 1/4-inch strips, then cut each slice into 1-inch pieces. Add to skillet and stir.

3/4 tsp. soy sauce

Add soy sauce and drained rice to skil-let with lid. Cook **1 minute (_____) at 100% power.** Slice cooked egg into 1-inch strips, then cut each slice into 1/8-inch pieces. Add to skillet and mix well. Cook **1 minute (_____) at 100% power** to heat. Put into small bowl and serve.

* Leftover Pork Roast (see recipe) is excellent in this dish.

VEGETABLES

ARTICHOKE

1 tsp. vinegar
3 cups water

Pour vinegar and water into 1-quart mixing bowl and set aside.

8-oz. artichoke

Cut off bottom stem and top 1-inch portion of artichoke with sharp knife. Cut off tips of leaves with kitchen shears. Soak artichoke in vinegar and water solution. Lift artichoke out of bowl and shake off excess liquid. Wrap in plastic wrap. Place artichoke upside-down on oven tray or bottom of oven. Cook **5:30 minutes (_____) at 100% power** until bottom leaves pull away easily from stem. Place on plate and serve.

TERIYAKI ARTICHOKE

8-oz. artichoke

Place artichoke on cutting surface and cut in half from top to bottom. Cut off bottom stem and top 1-inch portion of artichoke with sharp knife. Cut off tips of leaves with kitchen shears. Scoop out fuzzy center of each half with teaspoon.

2 cups water
1 tsp. vinegar

Pour water and vinegar into 1-quart mixing bowl. Soak artichoke halves in bowl. Remove from bowl and shake out excess liquid. Place halves in Menu-ette Skillet with cut side up and top ends together.

1/4 tsp. dried basil
2 tbsp. teriyaki sauce

Sprinkle each artichoke half with basil. Spread 1 tbsp. teriyaki sauce over each half. Cover with lid. Cook **6 minutes (_____) at 100% power** until leaves pull away easily from stem. Let stand **1 minute (_____)**. Serve in skillet.

ASPARAGUS

4 oz. fresh asparagus
1 tbsp. water

Wash asparagus and break into 1-inch pieces, discarding tough end pieces. Place in 1½-pint Menu-ette. Add water and cover with lid. Cook **3 minutes (_____) at 100% power.** Set aside until rest of meal is prepared.

1/16 tsp. salt
1 tsp. butter

Final preparation: Sprinkle asparagus with salt and stir. Drain and top with butter. Cook **30 seconds (_____) at 100% power** to heat before serving.

SPICY BAKED BEANS

1 slice bacon

Place bacon in 1-pint Menu-ette. Cover Menu-ette with paper towel. Cook **1 minute (_____) at 100% power** until bacon is crisp. Remove paper towel and place bacon on it to drain.

1 tsp. minced fresh or frozen onion

Place onion in bacon drippings in Menu-ette. Cook **20 seconds (_____) at 100% power.**

8-oz. can pork and beans, drained
1/2 tsp. brown sugar
1/2 tsp. molasses
1/4 tsp. Worcestershire sauce
1 tsp. ketchup

Add remaining ingredients to Menu-ette. Mix thoroughly with rubber spatula. Cover Menu-ette with lid. Cook **2:30 minutes (_____) at 100% power.*** Crumble cooked bacon. Add to Menu-ette and mix. Cover Menu-ette with lid. Let stand **1 minute (_____)** before serving or until rest of meal is prepared.

* For thicker beans, cook uncovered for **5 minutes (_____) at 50% power.**

GREEN BEANS

4 oz. fresh green beans
3 tbsp. water

Wash beans in water. Remove and discard ends of beans. Break beans into 1-inch pieces and place in 1½-pint Menu-ette. Add water. Cover Menu-ette with lid. Cook **6 minutes (_____) at 100% power** until beans are tender. Set aside until rest of meal is prepared.

1/8 tsp. salt
1 tsp. butter

Final preparation: Sprinkle beans with salt and stir. Drain off any liquid. Add butter and cover with lid. Cook **30 seconds (_____) at 100% power** to heat before serving.

Variation: Eliminate butter. After heating beans for serving, top with Supreme Cheese Sauce (see recipe).

LIMA BEANS

2 cups water
1/2 cup fresh lima beans

Pour water into Gravy Maker Pot or Cook 'N' Pour Pan. Cook **5 minutes (_____) at 100% power** until water boils. Wash lima beans and add to water. Cook **9 minutes (_____) at 100% power.**

1 cup water

Add water and cover with lid. Let stand **5 minutes (_____)** or until rest of meal is ready.

1/4 tsp. salt
1 tsp. butter

Final preparation: Add salt. Stir beans and drain. Add butter. Cook **30 seconds (_____) at 100% power** to heat before serving.

BROCCOLI

2 oz. fresh broccoli
1 tsp. water

Wash broccoli and cut into flowerets. Put pieces into 1½-pint Menu-ette. Sprinkle broccoli with water. Cover Menu-ette with lid. Cook **2 minutes (_____) at 100% power.** Set aside until rest of meal is prepared.

1/8 tsp. salt
1 tsp. lemon juice or butter

Final preparation: Sprinkle broccoli with salt and lemon juice. Cook **30 seconds (_____) at 100% power** to heat before serving.

CABBAGE

4 oz. fresh cabbage

Wash cabbage and cut into bite-size pieces. Place pieces in 1½-pint Menu-ette. Cover with lid. Cook **4 minutes (_____) at 100% power.** Set aside until rest of meal is prepared.

pinch of salt
1 tsp. butter

Final preparation: Sprinkle cabbage with salt and top with butter. Cook **30 seconds (_____) at 100% power** to heat before serving.

CARROTS

Note: When doubling this recipe, use a 1½-quart Corning Ware Visions saucepan so water will not boil over. Cook **10 minutes (_____) at 100% power.**

2 oz. thinly sliced fresh carrots **1/2 cup water**	Put carrots and water into Gravy Maker Pot or Cook 'N' Pour Pan. Cover pot with lid. Cook **8 minutes (_____) at 100% power.** Set aside until rest of meal is prepared.
1/8 tsp. salt **1 tsp. butter**	Final preparation: Sprinkle carrots with salt and mix with spoon. Drain off any water. Top carrots with butter and re-place lid. Cook **30 seconds (_____) at 100% power** to heat before serving.

CAULIFLOWER

3 oz. fresh cauliflower **1 tbsp. water**	Wash cauliflower and cut into bite-size pieces. Put pieces into 1½-pint Menu-ette. Add water and cover Menu-ette with lid. Cook **2:30 minutes (_____) at 100% power.** Set aside until rest of meal is prepared.
1/4 tsp. salt **1 tsp. butter**	Final preparation: Sprinkle cauliflower with salt and top with butter. Cook **30 seconds (_____) at 100% power** to heat before serving.

Variation: Eliminate salt and butter. Just before serving, place a slice of American cheese on top of cauliflower. Cook **30 seconds (_____) at 100% power** to melt cheese. Let stand **1 minute (_____)** before serving.

CORN ON THE COB

Note: Moisture will condense on oven tray when corn cooks. To avoid superheating the moisture and causing the tray to crack, always wipe the tray dry before putting a browning utensil in the oven.

9-oz. ear of corn in husk

Remove and discard dirty outer leaves of husk. Cut off bottom stem and immature top portion with strong knife. Place corn on oven tray or on bottom of oven. Cook **2 minutes (_____) at 100% power.** Turn corn over and rotate halfway around. Cook **1 minute (_____) at 100% power.** Wrap corn in 2 paper towels. Set aside until rest of meal is prepared.

Final preparation: Remove paper towels from corn. With a paper towel in each hand, strip husk from corn. Discard husks. Rub silk from corn with paper towels. Place corn in corn dish or other appropriate dish.

1 tbsp. butter

Put butter on top of corn. Cover corn dish with another corn dish or a piece of waxed paper. Cook **30 seconds (_____) at 100% power** to melt butter and heat corn. Roll corn in melted butter and serve.

MOMMA'S EGGPLANT PARMIGIANA

3-oz. eggplant
2 tbsp. milk
2 tbsp. all-purpose flour

Wash eggplant and cut into 1/4-inch slices (about 8 slices). Put milk into shallow bowl. Sprinkle flour on paper plate. Dip eggplant slices into milk, then into flour, coating slices entirely. Leave slices on plate and set aside.

1/4 cup vegetable oil
1 small peeled garlic clove

Put oil and garlic into 10" browning skillet. Prop up one corner of skillet with a small overturned dish or plastic jar lid so that oil collects on one side of skillet, covering garlic. Cook **3 minutes (_____) at 100% power.** Remove and discard garlic. Remove prop so skillet lies flat.

Heat skillet **2 minutes (_____) at 100% power.** Arrange eggplant slices in oil in one layer. Cook **1 minute (_____) at 100% power.** Turn slices over with finger tongs. Cook **1 minute (_____) at 100% power.** Remove slices and drain on paper towel. Set aside.

5 tbsp. (5 oz.) tomato sauce
1/2 tsp. oregano
2½ oz. grated Mozzarella cheese
1 tsp. grated Parmesan cheese

Pour off and discard excess oil in skillet. Add tomato sauce and oregano. Cover skillet with lid. Cook **2 minutes (_____) at 100% power.** Place 1 tbsp. sauce in 1½-pint Menu-ette. Arrange half of eggplant slices on top of sauce. Sprinkle half of Mozzarella cheese on top of eggplant. Cover with 1 tbsp. sauce. Repeat layers with remaining eggplant, Mozzarella cheese, and sauce. Sprinkle with Parmesan cheese. Cook **2 minutes (_____) at 100% power,** giving Menu-ette a half-turn halfway through cooking time. (Autorotating oven: Eliminate turn.) Let stand at least **1 minute (_____)** before serving or refrigerate and serve cold.

MOMMA'S STUFFED EGGPLANT

8-oz. eggplant
1/4 tsp. salt

Wash eggplant and cut off stem end. Cut eggplant in half lengthwise. Cut several long grooves into cut surface with a knife, being careful not to cut all the way through to skin. Sprinkle cut surface with salt. Put halves back together and wrap eggplant in paper towel. Cook **4 minutes (_____) at 100% power.** Place eggplant on counter, open paper towel, and separate halves to cool.

1/2 tsp. dried parsley or
  1 tsp. minced fresh or
  frozen parsley
1 tbsp. grated Romano cheese
1½ oz. grated Mozzarella
  cheese
1 small egg

When cool enough to handle, scoop out inside of eggplant halves with small spoon and place in small bowl. Add parsley, cheeses, and egg. Mix well. Fill each eggplant half with mixture and set aside.

1/4 cup vegetable oil
1 small peeled garlic clove

Put oil and garlic into 10″ browning skillet.* Prop up one corner of skillet with a small overturned dish or plastic jar lid so that oil collects on one side of skillet, covering garlic. Cook **4 minutes (_____) at 100% power.** Remove prop so skillet lies flat. Remove and discard garlic.

Using turner, carefully place eggplant in oil, stuffing side down. Repeat with other half. Cover skillet with microwave plastic dome cover. Cook **2 minutes (_____) at 100% power.** Remove eggplant with turner and place skin side down on paper towel to drain. Pour off and discard all but 1 tbsp. of oil in skillet.

(Continued on page 90)

8-oz. can tomato sauce
1/2 tsp. oregano
1/2 tsp. dried basil
1/2 tsp. dried parsley or
  1 tsp. minced fresh or
  frozen parsley
1 oz. grated Mozzarella
  cheese

Add tomato sauce and spices to oil and stir. Cover skillet with lid. Cook **2 minutes** (_____) at **100% power.** Place eggplant halves skin side down in skillet. Sprinkle eggplant with cheese and spoon sauce over all. Cook **2:30 minutes** (_____) at **100% power.** Cover skillet with lid. Let stand at least **1 minute** (_____) before serving.

* A large browning skillet is used in this recipe to make it easier to get eggplant in and out of skillet.

STUFFED MUSHROOMS

2 oz. mushrooms
1 tbsp. minced fresh or
  frozen onion
1 tsp. butter

Wash or brush mushrooms clean. Remove stems. Enlarge cavity in each mushroom cap with small knife, placing scrapings in small bowl. Chop up stems and add to bowl. Add onion and butter and mix. Cook **20 seconds** (_____) at **100% power.**

1 tbsp. dry bread crumbs
1 tsp. dried parsley or
  1 tbsp. minced fresh or
  frozen parsley
1/16 tsp. garlic salt
1/8 tsp. dry mustard

Add remaining ingredients and mix well. Place paper towel on paper plate and place mushroom caps in a circle on top. Stuff cavity of each cap with mixture. Cook **1:30 minutes** (_____) at **100% power,** giving plate a half-turn halfway through cooking time. (Autorotating oven: Eliminate turn.) Let stand **1 minute** (_____) before serving.

MUSHROOM LOAF

4 oz. mushrooms*

Wash or brush mushrooms clean and pat dry with paper towel. Chop fine and set aside.

1 tbsp. butter
1½ tbsp. (1/2 oz.) minced fresh or frozen onion
1½ tbsp. (1/2 oz.) minced celery

Place butter, onion, and celery in 1-pint Menu-ette. Cook **1:45 minutes** (_____) **at 100% power.** Set aside.

1 oz. cream cheese
1 small egg
3 tbsp. dry bread crumbs

Put cream cheese into small bowl. Cook **30 seconds** (_____) **at 100% power** until melted. Add egg and beat with wire whisk until smooth. Add mushrooms and onion mixture. Add bread crumbs and set aside.

1/4 tsp. salt
1/8 tsp. dried basil
1/16 tsp. rosemary
1/16 tsp. oregano
dash of black pepper

Grind spices together in small mortar and pestle. Add to mixture and mix well with rubber spatula, mashing mixture against sides of bowl. Pat mixture into 1½-cup refrigerator dish. Cover with lid. Cook **5 minutes** (_____) **at 100% power,** giving dish a half-turn halfway through cooking time. (Autorotating oven: Eliminate turn.) Turn out loaf onto plate. Let stand **2 minutes** (_____) before cutting into slices to serve. Serve as entree or chill and serve on sandwich.

* This recipe provides a delicious way to use up a large quantity of mushrooms or mushrooms that have lost their freshness.

PEAS

8 oz. fresh peas
1/3 cup water

Remove shells and place peas in 1½-pint Menu-ette. Add water and cover with lid. Cook **5 minutes** (_____) at **100% power.**

1/16 tsp. salt
1/2 tsp. sugar (optional)
1/4 cup water

Sprinkle peas with salt and sugar. Add water and mix. Cover with lid and set aside until rest of meal is prepared.

1 tsp. butter

Final preparation: Drain peas and add butter. Cover with lid. Cook **30 seconds** (_____) at **100% power** to heat before serving.

SNOW PEAS

4 oz. fresh snow peas
3 tbsp. water

Break off and discard both ends of each pea pod. If pods are stringy, remove and discard strings. Wash peas and place in 1½-pint Menu-ette. Add water and cover Menu-ette with lid. Cook **2:30 minutes** (_____) at **100% power** until peas are tender yet crisp. Set aside until rest of meal is prepared.

1/8 tsp. salt
1 tbsp. butter

Final preparation: Sprinkle with salt and stir Drain off any liquid. Add butter and cover. Cook **30 seconds** (_____) at **100% power** to heat before serving.

MOMMA'S ROASTED PEPPERS

8-oz. green pepper

Wash pepper and wrap in paper towel. Cook **4 minutes (_____) at 100% power.** Turn pepper over. Cook **4 minutes (_____) at 100% power** or until pepper skin is wrinkled. Put cooked pepper into small brown paper bag and fold end closed. Let stand **30 minutes (_____).**

1/16 tsp. salt
1/2 tsp. olive oil

Remove pepper from bag and place on cutting board. Peel off skin (it should peel away easily). Break or cut pepper open. Remove and discard stem and seeds. Tear pepper into strips and place in small bowl. Add salt and oil and mix well. Serve as is, as a salad, as filling for a sandwich, or chill in storage container and serve cold.

STUFFED BAKED POTATO

Note: When serving two people, use an 8-oz. potato and serve a half to each person.

Moisture will condense on the glass oven tray as potato cooks. To avoid superheating the moisture, which may cause tray to crack, always wipe tray dry before putting a browning utensil in the oven.

4-oz. baking potato

Scrub potato clean and pierce through with large two-tined fork. Place potato on oven tray or bottom of oven. Cook **1 minute (_____) at 100% power.** Turn potato over and halfway around. Cook **1 minute (_____) at 100% power** until potato is tender when pierced with toothpick. Cut potato in half lengthwise. Scoop out inside with small spoon and place in small bowl.

1/2 tbsp. butter
1½ tbsp. half and half
1/8 tsp. salt
dash of black pepper

Add butter, half and half, salt, and pepper to bowl. Mix with potato masher, then beat with wire whisk until creamy. Place potato skins in Menuette Skillet and fill with potato mixture.

1/4 oz. grated cheddar cheese
1/8 tsp. paprika

Sprinkle cheese over stuffed potato halves, then sprinkle with paprika. Set aside until rest of meal is prepared.

Final preparation: Cook **35 seconds (_____) at 100% power** until cheese melts. Let stand **1 minute (_____)** before serving.

POTATO WITH CHEESE

4-oz. baking potato
1/4 cup milk
1½ tbsp. (1 oz.) grated
 onion
1/2 tsp. all-purpose flour
1/4 tsp. salt

Peel and grate potato into 1-pint Menu ette. Add milk, onion, flour, and salt. Mix well. Cook **6 minutes (_____) at 100% power.**

1 oz. grated cheddar cheese
pinch of paprika

Add cheese and mix well. Sprinkle with paprika. Cook **2 minutes (_____) at 100% power.** Cover and let stand at least **1 minute (_____)** before serving.

PARSLIED POTATOES

4 oz. new potatoes

Choose potatoes that are of uniform size. Scrub potatoes clean. Place in 1-pint Menu-ette and cover with lid. Cook **2:30 minutes (_____) at 100% power** or until potatoes are tender when pierced with toothpick. Set aside.

2 tsp. butter
1/4 tsp. dried parsley
 or 1/2 tsp. minced fresh
 or frozen parsley

Place butter and parsley in custard cup. Cook **15 seconds (_____) at 100% power.** Set aside. Peel potatoes, discarding skins. Cut potatoes into quarters. Discard any liquid in Menu-ette and put potatoes back in. Add parsley and butter and toss with fork. Cover Menu-ette with lid and set aside until rest of meal is prepared.

Final preparation: Cook **30 seconds (_____) at 100% power** to heat before serving.

WHIPPED POTATOES

6-oz. baking potato
1/2 cup water
1/4 tsp. salt

Peel potato and cut into 1/2-inch cubes. Put into 1-quart Corning Ware pot. Add water and cover pot with lid. Cook **6 minutes (_____) at 100% power** or until potato is tender when pierced with toothpick. Add salt and stir. Replace lid and set aside until rest of meal is almost done. Pour off water into container and save to use in gravy for roast (see recipe).

1 tsp. butter
1½ tbsp. sour cream

Add butter and sour cream to potatoes. Mash mixture with potato masher to eliminate lumps, then beat with electric mixer until potatoes are creamy. Replace lid and set aside until rest of meal is prepared.

Final preparation: Cook **45 seconds (_____) at 100% power** to heat potatoes. Stir before serving.

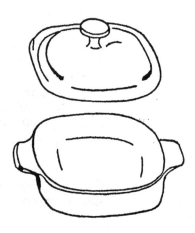

RUTABAGA

1 slice bacon

Place paper towel on paper plate. Place bacon on one half of paper towel and fold other half over bacon. Cook **1 minute (_____) at 100% power** until done, but not crisp. Set aside.

6-oz. rutabaga
1/2 cup water

Peel and wash rutabaga. Cut into 1/2-inch cubes and place in Cook 'N' Pour Pan. Add water and cover with lid. Cook **5:30 minutes (_____) at 100% power** until rutabaga is tender when pierced with toothpick.

1/8 tsp. salt
1 tsp. butter

Sprinkle with salt and stir well. Cover and let stand **1 minute (_____).** Pour off water. Mash rutabaga with potato masher. Add butter and mix well. Cut bacon into 1/2-inch pieces and add to rutabaga. Cover pan with lid. Set aside until rest of meal is prepared.

Final preparation: Cook **30 seconds (_____) at 100% power** to heat before serving.

SPINACH

**4 oz. washed fresh spinach*
or rappini**

Stuff spinach into 1½-pint Menu-ette and cover with lid. Cook **4 minutes (_____) at 100% power** until tender. Set aside until rest of meal is prepared.

**1/8 tsp. salt
2 tsp. butter**

Final preparation: Sprinkle spinach with salt and mix. Drain spinach in strainer, pressing out excess liquid with rubber spatula. Return spinach to Menu-ette. Top with butter and cover with lid. Cook **45 seconds (_____) at 100% power** to heat before serving.

* If spinach is bought loose, start with 6 oz.; if bought in a 1-pound plastic package, the yield of clean spinach can be 4 -14 oz.
To obtain 4 oz. washed fresh spinach, start with about 6 oz. fresh spinach. Remove the bad leaves and the tough stems. Place spinach in sink and fill with water. Swish water around to dislodge sand, then allow sand to settle at bottom, leaving spinach floating. Scoop up spinach with your hands or a strainer.

SQUASH

**4-oz. thin-skinned yellow
squash
2-oz. onion**

Scrub squash gently. Cut off ends and slice thinly into 1-pint Menu-ette. Peel and slice onion thinly and place slices over squash. Cover Menu-ette with lid. Cook **4 minutes (_____) at 100% power.** Set aside until rest of meal is prepared.

**1/8 tsp. salt
pinch of black pepper
(optional)
1 tsp. butter**

Final preparation: Sprinkle with salt and pepper. Mix well with fork. Top with butter and cover with lid. Cook **1 minute (_____) at 100% power** to heat before serving.

Variation: Substitute thinly sliced green pepper for the onion.

SQUASH CASSEROLE

**3-oz. thin-skinned yellow
  squash**
**1 tbsp. chopped fresh or
  frozen onion**
1 tsp. butter

Wash squash and grate into 1-quart mixing bowl. Add onion and butter. Cover bowl with paper towel. Cook **2 minutes (_____) at 100% power.**

1 tsp. sugar
1/8 tsp. salt
1/16 tsp. black pepper
**1/2 oz. crushed saltine
  crackers (4 crackers)**
1 small egg, beaten
1/4 tsp. baking powder
**1 tbsp. instant nonfat dry
  milk* (optional)**

Add remaining ingredients and mix well. Pour mixture into greased 14-oz. Pyrex Bake Mate. Cook **40 seconds (_____) at 100% power.** Turn bowl halfway around. Cook **45 seconds (_____) at 100% power.** Cover and let stand at least **1 minute (_____)** before serving.

* Adding dry milk makes the casserole tastier and more nutritious.

WHIPPED SWEET POTATO

6-oz. sweet potato

Wash sweet potato and dry with paper towel. Pierce with large two-tined fork. Place on oven tray or bottom of oven. Cook **2 minutes (_____) at 100% power.** Turn potato over. Cook **1 minute (_____) at 100% power** or until potato is tender when pierced with toothpick. Wrap potato in aluminum foil and set aside for **5 minutes (_____).**

2 tsp. butter
1 tbsp. milk

Remove foil. Peel and discard skin. Place potato in 1-quart mixing bowl. Add butter and mash with electric mixer beaters. Then beat with mixer on high speed until well blended. Add milk and beat with mixer until creamy. Set aside until rest of meal is prepared.

Final preparation: Cook **1 minute (_____) at 100% power** to heat before serving.

CANDIED YAMS

3 tbsp. brown sugar
1½ tbsp. butter
2 tbsp. water or liquid from yams

8-oz. can yams or sweet potatoes or 8-oz. fresh yam or sweet potato

Place sugar, butter and water in 1-cup liquid measure. Cook **45 seconds** (_____) **at 100% power** until contents are dissolved. Stir and set aside.

If using fresh yam, scrub and pierce with large two-tined fork. Cook **3 minutes** (_____) **at 100% power** until potato is tender when pierced with toothpick. Remove and discard skin. Cut yam into 1/2-inch slices. Place yam slices or canned yams in Menu-ette Skillet. Pour sugar mixture over yams. Cover skillet with lid. Cook **8 minutes** (_____) **at 50% power.** Set aside until rest of meal is prepared.

Final preparation: Cook **30 seconds** (_____) **at 100% power** to heat before serving.

FROZEN VEGETABLES

Asparagus:

4 oz. frozen asparagus

Separate asparagus spears with blunt table knife. Place asparagus in Menu-ette Skillet and cover with lid. Cook **2:30 minutes (_____) at 100% power.** Set aside until rest of meal is prepared.

1/16 tsp. salt
1 tbsp. butter

Final preparation: Sprinkle asparagus with salt and top with butter. Cook **30 seconds (_____) at 100% power** to heat before serving.

Broccoli, Cauliflower, Corn, Green Beans:

2 oz. (1/2 cup) frozen broccoli, cauliflower, whole kernel corn, or green beans
1 tbsp. water

Place vegetable and water in 1-pint Menu-ette and cover with lid. Cook **3 minutes (_____) at 100% power.** Set aside until rest of meal is prepared.

1/8 tsp. salt
1 tsp. butter

Final preparation: Sprinkle vegetable with salt and stir. Drain off any liquid. Top vegetable with butter and cover with lid. Cook **30 seconds (_____) at 100% power** to heat before serving.

Butter Beans, Lima Beans:

2 oz. (1/2 cup) frozen butter beans or lima beans
1/4 cup water

Place vegetables and water in Gravy Maker Pot or Cook 'N' Pour Pan. Cover with lid. Cook **4 minutes (_____) at 100% power.**

1/8 tsp. salt
1/4 cup warm water

Add salt and warm water. Stir. Cover and let stand until rest of meal is prepared.

1 tsp. butter

Final preparation: Drain off liquid. Top vegetables with butter and replace lid. Cook **30 seconds (_____) at 100% power** to heat before serving.

Carrots, Mixed Vegetables:

Note: When doubling this recipe, cooking time and power remain the same.

2 oz. (1/2 cup) frozen sliced carrots, whole baby carrots, or mixed vegetables
1/3 cup water

Place vegetables and water in Gravy Maker Pot or Cook 'N' Pour Pan. Cover with lid. Cook **6 minutes (_____) at 100% power** until vegetables are tender. Set aside until rest of meal is prepared.

1/8 tsp. salt
1 tsp. butter

Final preparation: Sprinkle with salt and stir. Drain off any liquid. Top vegetables with butter and replace lid. Cook **30 seconds (_____) at 100% power** to heat before serving.

Peas:

2 oz. (1/2 cup) frozen peas
1 tbsp. water

Put peas and water into 1-pint Menuette and cover with lid. Cook **3 minutes (_____) at 100% power** until tender.

1/8 tsp. salt
1/4 cup warm water

Sprinkle peas with salt and add warm water. Stir and cover with lid. Set aside until rest of meal is prepared.

1 tsp. butter

Final preparation: Drain off any liquid. Top peas with butter and replace lid. Cook **30 seconds (_____) at 100% power** to heat before serving.

Spinach:

4 oz. (1 cup) frozen chopped spinach

Place spinach in 1½-pint Menu-ette. Cover with lid. Cook **3 minutes (_____) at 100% power** until tender. Set aside until rest of meal is prepared.

1/8 tsp. salt
2 tsp. butter

Final preparation: Add salt and stir. Squeeze out excess liquid with fork. Top spinach with butter and replace lid. Cook **45 seconds (_____) at 100% power** to heat. Mix well before serving.

Note: To double this recipe, cook a 10-oz. package of leaf or chopped spinach right in its cardboard container. Remove outer wrapping and cook spinach as below. After standing time, squeeze out excess liquid, place in Menu-ette, add butter and heat before serving.

SAUCES AND PRESERVES

APPLESAUCE

Note: Applesauce is a great accompaniment for Pork Roast (see recipe).

6-oz. apple
1/4 cup water
2 whole cloves
1½ tsp. light brown sugar

Peel and quarter apple and remove core. Cut into 1/2-inch cubes. Place in 1½-pint Menu-ette.* Add water and cloves. Cover Menu-ette with lid. Cook **6 minutes (_____) at 100% power.** Remove and discard cloves. Mash mixture with potato masher. Cook **1 minute (_____) at 100% power.** Add sugar, stir, and serve.

* When doubling recipe, cook in Gravy Maker Pot to avoid applesauce boiling over.

SPICY BARBECUE SAUCE

2 tbsp. bottled barbecue sauce
1 tsp. corn syrup
1/2 tsp. Worcestershire sauce
1/4 tsp. lemon juice
1 drop Tabasco sauce
1/8 tsp. minced fresh or frozen garlic
1½ tsp. minced fresh or frozen onion

Place ingredients in 1-cup liquid measure. Cook **1 minute (_____) at 100% power.** Pour over meat during last cooking step.

SWEET AND SPICY BARBECUE SAUCE

1 tsp. vegetable oil
1 tbsp. dry sherry
1 tbsp. water
1 tbsp. raisins
1 tsp. sugar
1/4 tsp. salt
dash of black pepper
pinch of ground cloves
1/8 tsp. minced fresh or
   frozen garlic
2 tsp. minced fresh or
   frozen onion

Place ingredients in 1-cup liquid measure. Cook **1 minute** (_____) at **100% power.** Pour over meat during last cooking step.

SOUTHERN BARBECUE SAUCE

1 tsp. vegetable oil
2 tsp. lemon juice
2 tbsp. ketchup
2 tbsp. cider vinegar
1 tbsp. honey
2 tsp. Worcestershire sauce
1/4 tsp. dry mustard
1/8 tsp. ground ginger
1/8 tsp. salt
1/8 tsp. minced fresh or
   frozen garlic
2 tsp. minced fresh or
   frozen onion

Place ingredients in 1-cup liquid measure. Cook **1 minute** (_____) at **100% power.** Pour over meat during last cooking step.

INSTANT CHEESE SAUCE

3/4 oz. grated Gruyere
  cheese
2 tbsp. sour cream
dash of salt

Mix ingredients in custard cup. Spread on fish, baked potato, or cooked vegetable. Cook **30 seconds** (_____) **at 100% power** to melt cheese.

SUPREME CHEESE SAUCE

1 tsp. milk
1 tsp. cream cheese
1/2 tsp. grated Parmesan
  cheese
dash of onion salt

Place milk and cream cheese in custard cup. Cook **20 seconds** (_____) at **100% power.** Stir mixture with wire whisk until smooth. Add remaining ingredients and stir well with whisk. Serve over cooked vegetables in place of butter.

CRANBERRY SAUCE

1 oz. fresh or frozen
  cranberries*
2 tbsp. sugar
1 tbsp. water

Wash and coarsely chop cranberries. Place in 1-quart mixing bowl. Add sugar and water and mix well. Cover bowl with lid or a piece of waxed paper. Cook **1:30 minutes** (_____) at **100% power.** Pour sauce into custard cup to serve.

* If fresh cranberries are prepackaged in a plastic bag, freeze unused portion in same bag. To cook cranberries, do not thaw; just rinse in cold water before cooking.

MORNAY SAUCE

1 tsp. butter
1 tsp. all-purpose flour
2 tbsp. water

Place butter in 1-pint Menu-ette. Cook **10 seconds (_____) at 100% power** until melted. Add flour and water. Mix well with wire whisk. Cook **20 seconds (_____) at 100% power** until mixture boils.

1/2 tbsp. shredded Swiss cheese
1/2 tbsp. grated Parmesan cheese

Add cheeses. Cook **15 seconds (_____) at 100% power** to melt cheese. Serve over cooked green vegetables.

PASTA SAUCE

1/2 tsp. olive oil
1½ oz. lean ground beef
1½ oz. Italian sausage*
1/16 tsp. minced fresh or frozen garlic
1/16 tsp. black pepper
1 tbsp. unfrozen or frozen tomato paste

Place oil, ground beef, sausage (with casing removed), and garlic in Gravy Maker Pot or Cook 'N' Pour Pan. Cook **1 minute (_____) at 100% power**. Add pepper and tomato paste. (If tomato paste is frozen, stir in hot mixture until it melts.)

6 oz. tomato sauce or 6 oz. fresh or canned whole tomato**
1/2 tsp. dried basil or 1 fresh basil leaf
1 serving of macaroni (see recipe)

Add tomato and basil. Cover pot with lid. Cook **4 minutes (_____) at 100% power**. Stir well and replace lid. Cook **4 minutes (_____) at 50% power**. Set aside. Cook and drain macaroni. Pour sauce over macaroni and serve.

* Ground veal or more ground beef may be substituted for sausage.
** If fresh or canned whole tomato is used, increase amount of tomato paste in first step to 2 tbsp.

VEGETARIAN PASTA SAUCE

1 tbsp. vegetable oil

Pour oil into 8½" browning skillet. Cook **4 minutes (_____) at 100% power.**

4 oz. peeled eggplant, cut into 1/2-inch cubes
6 tbsp. (6 oz.) tomato sauce
1/8 tsp. oregano
1/8 tsp. dried basil
dash of red pepper
1 serving of macaroni (see recipe)

Spread eggplant evenly in skillet. Cook **1 minute (_____) at 100% power.** Turn eggplant over with turner. Cook **1 minute (_____) at 100% power.** Add tomato sauce and spices to skillet and cover with lid. Cook **4 minutes (_____) at 100% power.** Stir and replace lid. Cook **2 minutes (_____) at 50% power.** Set aside. Cook and drain macaroni. Pour sauce over macaroni and serve.

About preserves:

Before I started using a microwave oven, I thought it was wasteful to buy a whole box of strawberries or blueberries because I could not eat them all by myself. Now I can enjoy a bowl of strawberries and cream or make Blueberry Streusel Cake (see recipe) and turn the leftover fruit into easy microwave preserves. The reduced amount of sugar in these recipes brings out the taste of the fruit.

It's easy to adjust a recipe for microwave preserves, which is fortunate because the amount of pectin needed varies with the condition and type of fruit used. If the jar of preserves does not jell after being thoroughly chilled, just put the preserves back into a bowl, add 1/4 tsp. pectin, heat to boiling, and rechill. If the preserves turn out too thick, add 2 tbsp. water and mix well. It is important to chill the preserves before covering with a lid, as specified in the instructions, because even in the refrigerator bacteria will grow when hot air is trapped between the food and the cover.

BLUEBERRY PRESERVES

8 oz. (1 cup) fresh blueberries*

Wash blueberries and remove stems before measuring. Place blueberries in 2-quart mixing bowl with handle.

2 tsp. powdered pectin

Add pectin and stir. Cover bowl with a piece of waxed paper. Cook **2 minutes (_____) at 100% power** until mixture boils.

1/2 cup sugar

Add sugar and stir well. Replace waxed paper. Cook **4 minutes (_____) at 100% power** until mixture thickens. Pour into clean 10-oz. jar. Place jar, uncovered, in refrigerator. When preserves are completely chilled, cover with lid and store in refrigerator.

* If blueberries are frozen, increase the first cooking time to **4 minutes (_____) at 100% power.** The rest of the recipe remains the same.

PEACH PRESERVES

12 oz. ripe peaches

Peel peaches. Cut each peach in half all around pit, then twist halves in opposite directions. Pit should then be easy to remove and discard. Cut into 1/2-inch cubes and place in 2-quart mixing bowl.

3½ tsp. powdered pectin

Add pectin. Cover bowl with a piece of waxed paper. Cook **2:30 minutes (_____) at 100% power.** Stir mixture and replace waxed paper. Cook **1 minute (_____) at 100% power.**

2/3 cup sugar

Add sugar and stir well. Replace waxed paper. Cook **1:30 minutes (_____) at 100% power.** Scrape mixture down from sides of bowl and stir. Replace waxed paper. Cook **1:30 minutes (_____) at 100% power.** Pour into clean 10-oz. jar. Place jar, uncovered, in refrigerator. When preserves are completely chilled, cover jar with lid and store in refrigerator.

ITALIAN PLUM PRESERVES

8 oz. Italian purple plums (prune plums)

Wash plums, cut in half, and discard pits. Place in blender or food processor and liquify. (If blender is not available, chop plums as fine as possible.)

2¾ tsp. powdered pectin

Pour contents of blender into 1-quart mixing bowl. Add pectin and mix well. Cover bowl with a piece of waxed paper. Cook **3 minutes (_____) at 100% power** until mixture boils. Remove and discard waxed paper.

1/2 cup sugar

Add sugar and mix well. Cook **2 minutes (_____) at 100% power.** Scrape mixture down from sides of bowl and stir. Cook **1 minute (_____) at 100% power.** Pour into clean 10-oz. jar. Put jar, uncovered, into refrigerator. When preserves are completely chilled, cover jar with lid and store in refrigerator.

Variation: Apricots can be used in this recipe. No blender is needed. Pit apricots, then chop into 1/2-inch pieces and follow recipe as given above.

STRAWBERRY PRESERVES

8 oz. fresh strawberries*

Wash strawberries and remove stems before weighing. Place berries in 2-quart mixing bowl.

1 tbsp. powdered pectin

Add pectin and stir. Cover bowl with a piece of waxed paper. Cook **2:30 minutes (_____) at 100% power.** Stir with rubber spatula. Replace waxed paper. Cook **30 seconds (_____) at 100% power** until mixture boils.

2/3 cup sugar

Add sugar and stir. Cook **1:30 minutes (_____) at 100% power.** Scrape mixture down from sides of bowl and stir. Cook **3 minutes (_____) at 50% power.** Stir with spatula and pour into clean 10-oz. jar. Place jar, uncovered, in refrigerator. When preserves are completely chilled, cover jar with lid and store in refrigerator.

* If strawberries are frozen, increase the first cooking time to **4:30 minutes (_____) at 100% power.** The rest of the recipe stays the same.

MARMALADE

1¼ cups water
1½ cups sugar
1/16 tsp. baking soda

Place water, sugar, and baking soda in 2-quart mixing bowl. Set aside.

6-oz. orange
3-oz. lemon

Wash orange and lemon. Peel outer skin of each into strips with potato peeler. Cut across strips to make 1/16-inch shavings. Add to bowl and stir. Cook **5 minutes (_____) at 100% power.** Remove white skin on orange and lemon with sharp knife and discard. Pull flesh of fruit apart onto plate section by section with knife, discarding all pits, membranes, and pulp. Scrape flesh and juice into bowl with rubber spatula.

3 tbsp. powdered pectin

Add pectin and mix well. Cook **10 minutes (_____) at 100% power.** Stir, then pour marmalade into clean 20-oz. jar. Place jar, uncovered, in refrigerator. When marmalade is completely chilled, cover jar with lid and store in refrigerator.

SALADS

CABBAGE SLAW

Note: Slaw will keep over a week stored in a jar in refrigerator.

4 oz. cabbage
1 tbsp. finely chopped
green pepper
1 tbsp. minced fresh or
frozen onion
1 tbsp. sugar

Shred cabbage into thin strips with sharp knife. Place in 1-quart mixing bowl and wash. Drain on paper towel. Return cabbage to emptied bowl. Add green pepper, onion, and sugar. Mix well and set aside.

4 tsp. vegetable oil
4 tsp. cider vinegar
1½ tsp. sugar
1/4 tsp. celery seed
1/4 tsp. salt

Place remaining ingredients in 1-pint Menu-ette. Cook **1 minute (_____)** **at 100% power.** Pour hot mixture over cabbage immediately. Mix well with rubber spatula. Chill for several hours before serving.

POTATO SALAD

4 oz. new potatoes

Choose potatoes that are of uniform size. Wash potatoes and place in 1-pint Menu-ette. Cover with lid. Cook **2 minutes (_____) at 100% power.** Cool potatoes enough to handle. Peel potatoes, then cut into halves and cut halves into thin slices. Place in small bowl.

1/4 cup mayonnaise
1 tbsp. chopped green pepper
1/8 tsp. salt
dash of white pepper

Add remaining ingredients and mix well. Chill before serving.

GERMAN HOT POTATO SALAD

4 oz. new potatoes

Peel potatoes and cut in half. Cut halves into 1/4-inch-thick slices. Set aside.

2 tbsp. water
1/8 tsp. salt

Place water, salt, and potatoes in 1-pint Menu-ette. Cover with lid. Cook **4 minutes (_____) at 100% power**, giving Menu-ette a half-turn halfway through cooking time. (Autorotating oven: Eliminate turn.) Remove lid and place upside down on counter. Put potatoes in upturned lid to cool.

1 slice bacon

Wipe emptied Menu-ette with paper towel. Put bacon in and cover with paper towel. Cook **1 minute (_____) at 100% power** until crisp. Remove bacon and place on paper towel to drain.

1/2 tbsp. chopped fresh or frozen onion

Add onion to bacon drippings in Menu-ette. Cook **45 seconds (_____) at 100% power.**

1/2 tbsp. sugar
1/4 tsp. celery seed
1 tsp. all-purpose flour
1/16 tsp. salt
dash of black pepper
2 tbsp. water
1/2 tsp. white vinegar

Add remaining ingredients and mix well with rubber spatula. Cook **55 seconds (_____) at 100% power**. Add potatoes to Menu-ette and mix. Cook **45 seconds (_____) at 100% power**. Crumble bacon and sprinkle on top of salad before serving.

MOMMA'S SHRIMP SALAD

1 cup water
1/2 tsp. salt
1/2 tsp. vegetable oil
3 tbsp. rice

Pour water into 1-quart Corning Ware pot. Cook **2:30 minutes (_____)** **at 100% power** until water boils. Add salt, oil, and rice. Spread evenly in pot. Cook **30 minutes (_____) at 30% power.** Drain in strainer. Put strainer into refrigerator to cool rice.

3 oz. fresh shrimp
1/4 tsp. Old Bay Seasoning
or other Chesapeake
Bay-style seafood
seasoning
1/8 tsp. salt

Wash shrimp and arrange on paper plate. Sprinkle shrimp with spices. Cook **1 minute (_____) at 100% power** until tails curl and shrimp turn pink. Set aside to cool.

3 tbsp. (1 oz.) chopped
celery
1/8 tsp. white pepper
3 tbsp. mayonnaise

Empty rice into small bowl and add remaining ingredients. Peel and devein shrimp. Cut into 1/2-inch pieces and add to bowl. Mix well with rubber spatula. Chill before serving.

CRANBERRY GELATIN

2 oz. fresh or frozen
cranberries*
1/4 cup water
1/2 tsp. unflavored gelatin
2 tbsp. sugar

Wash cranberries. Place in blender and chop on highest setting. Add remaining ingredients and blend. Pour mixture into 1-quart bowl and cover with lid or waxed paper. Cook **2 minutes (_____) at 100% power.** Pour into custard cup and chill until firm. Serve in custard cup or unmold onto plate.

* If fresh cranberries are prepackaged in a plastic bag, freeze unused portion in same bag. To cook cranberries, do not thaw; just rinse in cold water and cook.

FISH AND SHELLFISH

Note: The fish recipes in this section use either fresh or frozen fish. If you don't get good results with one brand of frozen fish, try another brand. Sea Pak is one brand that cooks up as well as fresh fish. To test whether a product will be good for microwave cooking, defrost a 3-oz. fillet for **2 minutes (_____) at 30% power,** then place in a Menu-ette Skillet, sprinkle lightly with salt and pepper, and cook **1:30 minutes (_____) at 100% power** until done. If the fish isn't good cooked this simply, it will not be good cooked any other way.

FISH FILLET WITH BREAD CRUMBS

1½ tsp. butter
1/4 tsp. dried parsley or
  3/4 tsp. minced fresh or
  frozen parsley
1/8 tsp. tarragon, dill
  weed, or thyme
1/8 tsp. onion salt
pinch of nutmeg

Put butter into custard cup. Cook **30 seconds (_____) at 100% power** until melted. Add parsley, tarragon, onion salt, and nutmeg and mix. Set aside.

4-oz. fresh or frozen fish
  fillet

If fish is frozen, defrost **2 minutes (_____) at 30% power.** Rinse off fillet with water and pat dry with paper towel. Spread 1/8 tsp. spice mixture on the skin side of the fish (on either side if there is no skin). Place fish in Menu-ette Skillet, coated side down.

2 tbsp. dry bread crumbs

Add bread crumbs to remaining spice mixture in custard cup and mix well with small fork. Sprinkle over top of fillet and cover skillet with paper towel. Cook **2 minutes (_____) at 100% power.** Let stand **1 minute (_____)** before serving.

MOMMA'S BREADED FISH

4-oz. fresh or frozen fish fillet
1/16 tsp. salt
1/16 tsp. black pepper

If fish is frozen, defrost **2 minutes (_____) at 30% power.** Rinse off fillet with water and pat dry with paper towel. Place fish in Casser-ette or Menu-ette Skillet. Sprinkle with salt and pepper. Set aside.

1 tbsp. Italian bread crumbs
1 tsp. olive oil
1 tsp. lemon juice

Put bread crumbs and olive oil into custard cup and mix well. Spread evenly over fillet and cover dish with paper towel. Cook **2 minutes (_____) at 100% power.** Sprinkle with lemon juice and serve.

FRIED FISH

4-oz. fresh or frozen fish fillet

If fish is frozen, defrost **2 minutes (_____) at 30% power.** Rinse off fillet with water and pat dry with paper towel. Set aside.

1 tbsp. milk
1 tbsp. all-purpose flour
1/8 tsp. salt
1/16 tsp. black pepper

Pour milk into shallow bowl. Mix flour, salt, and pepper on paper plate. Soak fillet in milk, then dredge in flour mixture. Leave on paper plate and set aside.

2 tbsp. vegetable oil
lemon wedge (optional)

Pour oil into 8½" browning skillet. Heat **2:30 minutes (_____) at 100% power.** Place fish in skillet and cover with paper towel. Cook **30 seconds (_____) at 100% power.** Remove and discard paper towel. Turn fish over with finger tongs. Cook **40 seconds (_____) at 100% power.** Drain fish on paper towel. Serve on plate with lemon.

BATTER-FRIED FISH

4-oz. fresh or frozen fish fillet
1 tbsp. all-purpose flour

If fish is frozen, defrost **2 minutes (_____) at 30% power.** Cut fish into 2-inch triangles. Rinse off with water and dry pieces well with paper towel. Spread flour on paper plate. Dredge fish in flour and leave on plate. Set aside.

1/4 cup vegetable oil

Pour oil into 8½″ browning skillet. Cook **6 minutes (_____) at 100% power.**

1/4 cup all-purpose flour
1/4 tsp. baking powder
1/4 tsp. sugar
1/8 tsp. salt
1/4 cup beer or club soda

While oil is heating, mix remaining ingredients in cereal bowl until mixture has the consistency of buttermilk. Coat each piece of fish with mixture and put back on plate. When oil is ready, place fish in skillet and cover with paper towel. Cook **40 seconds (_____) at 100% power.** Remove and discard paper towel. Turn fish over with finger tongs. Cook **30 seconds (_____) at 100% power.** Drain on paper towel, then serve on plate.

LEMON-BATTER FISH

3 oz. fresh or frozen white fish
1 tbsp. all-purpose flour

If fish is frozen, defrost **1:45 minutes** (_____) **at 30% power.** Rinse off with water and drain on paper towel. (Fish may be cooked in one piece or several small pieces.) Spread flour on paper plate. Dredge fish in flour. Leave on plate and set aside.

1/4 cup all-purpose flour
2½ tbsp. water
1 tbsp. lemon juice
1 small egg
1/8 tsp. sugar
1/8 tsp. salt
1/4 tsp. baking powder

Mix flour, water, lemon juice, egg, sugar, salt, and baking powder in shallow bowl. Coat fish with batter. Leave in bowl and set aside.

1/4 cup vegetable oil

Pour oil into 8½" browning skillet. Cook **5:30 minutes** (_____) **at 100% power.** Lift fish out of batter with finger tongs and place in oil. Cook **20 seconds** (_____) **at 100% power.** Turn fish over with finger tongs. Cook **30 seconds** (_____) **at 100% power.** Place fish on plate and serve.

CHEDDAR FISH FILLET

4 oz. fresh or frozen fish fillet

If fish is frozen, defrost **2 minutes (_____) at 30% power.** Rinse off fillet with water and pat dry with paper towel. Cut fillet into 3-inch squares and set aside.

2 tbsp. vegetable oil
1/8 tsp. salt
dash of black pepper
1/8 tsp. minced fresh or frozen garlic
3 tbsp. cracker crumbs or corn flake crumbs

Combine oil, salt, pepper, and garlic in shallow bowl. Place crumbs on a 12-inch piece of waxed paper and set aside. Dip fish pieces into oil mixture, then into crumbs. Place in Menu-ette Skillet.

1/2 oz. grated cheddar cheese

Sprinkle cheese over fish. Cover skillet with paper towel. Cook **1 minute (_____) at 100% power.** Set aside.

2 tbsp. ketchup

Put ketchup into 1-cup liquid measure and cover with paper towel. Cook **1 minute (_____) at 100% power.** Spread 1 tbsp. ketchup on cooked fish. Cover skillet with paper towel. Cook **1 minute (_____) at 100% power.** Place fish on plate and serve with remaining ketchup.

PARMESAN FISH FILLET

4-oz. fresh or frozen fish
fillet
1/8 tsp. black pepper

If fish is frozen, defrost **2 minutes**
(_____) at **30% power.** Rinse off
fillet with water and pat dry with paper
towel. Place fish in Casser-ette or Menu-
ette Skillet and sprinkle with pepper.
Set aside.

2 tbsp. mayonnaise
1 tbsp. stiffly beaten egg
white*
1/2 tsp. crushed dried
chives
1 tsp. grated Parmesan
cheese

Mix mayonnaise, egg white, and chives
in custard cup. Spread on top of fish
with small spatula. Sprinkle cheese over
fish. Cover skillet with paper towel. Cook
2 minutes (_____) at **100% power.** Let stand **1 minute** (_____).
Place on plate and serve.

* The egg yolk and remaining stiffly beaten egg white can be used in Fluffy Vanilla
Pudding or Fluffy Chocolate Pudding (see recipes).

FISH FILLET WITH TOMATO

4-oz. fresh or frozen
fish fillet
1/4 tsp. salt
1/8 tsp. black pepper

If fish is frozen, defrost **2 minutes**
(_____) at **30% power.** Rinse off
fish with water and pat dry with paper
towel. Sprinkle fish with salt and pepper and place in Casser-ette. Set aside.

1 tsp. butter
4 tsp. milk
1/4 tsp. all-purpose flour
4 tsp. dry white wine
1/8 tsp. dried basil

Put butter in 1-pint Menu-ette. Cook
20 seconds (_____) at **100% power** until melted. Mix in milk and flour.
Cook **20 seconds** (_____) at **100%
power.** Add wine and basil to Menu-
ette. Mix well.

2 oz. sliced tomato

Place tomato on top of fish and pour
sauce over all. Cook **2 minutes**
(_____) at **100% power,** giving
Casser-ette a half-turn halfway through
cooking time. (Autorotating oven: Eliminate turn.) Let stand **2 minutes**
(_____). Place on plate and serve.

FLOUNDER WITH STUFFING

1 tsp. butter

Place butter in Casser-ette or Menu-ette Skillet. Cook **20 seconds** (_____) **at 100% power** until melted. Set aside.

4-oz. fresh or frozen flounder or other fillet
1/8 tsp. salt
1/16 tsp. black pepper

If fish is frozen, defrost **2 minutes** (_____) **at 30% power.** Rinse off fillet with water and pat dry with paper towel. Place in Casser-ette and coat one side with melted butter. Turn fillet over with slotted turner and sprinkle with salt and pepper. Set aside.

1½ tsp. butter
2 tsp. chopped fresh or frozen onion
2 tsp. chopped shallot or green onion
1 tsp. chopped fresh or frozen green pepper
2 tsp. chopped celery
1/8 tsp. minced fresh or frozen garlic
1/4 tsp. all-purpose flour
2 tsp. dry white wine
2 tsp. milk

Mix butter and vegetables in 1½-pint Menu-ette. Cook **1 minute** (_____) **at 100% power.** Add flour, wine, and milk. Cook **1 minute** (_____) **at 100% power** until thick. Set aside.

3/4 oz. frozen crabmeat

Defrost crabmeat **1:30 minutes** (_____) **at 30% power.** Squeeze out excess water and set aside.

3/4 oz. fresh or frozen shrimp (3 medium shrimp)

If using fresh shrimp, wash, peel, and devein. Place shrimp on paper plate. Cook **30 seconds** (_____) **at 100% power** until pink. Chop shrimp into 1/2-inch pieces and add to Menu-ette.

(Continued on page 126)

2 tsp. dry bread crumbs
1/8 tsp. dried parsley or
1/2 tsp. minced fresh or
frozen parsley
2 tsp. beaten egg (optional)

Add crabmeat and remaining ingredients to Menu-ette. Mix thoroughly for several minutes with rubber spatula. Pat stuffing evenly over top of fish. Cover Casser-ette with lid. Cook **1 minute (_____) at 100% power.** Remove cover and turn Casser-ette halfway around. Cook **1 minute (_____) at 100% power.** Let stand **2 minutes (_____)** and serve.

FLOUNDER SWISS

4 oz. fresh or frozen
flounder or other fillet

If fish is frozen, defrost **2 minutes (_____) at 30% power.** Rinse off fillet with water and pat dry with paper towel.

1/4 tsp. Season-All salt
1/2 oz. grated or diced
Swiss cheese
2 oz. sliced tomato

Sprinkle fillet with Season-All. Place in Casser-ette or Menu-ette Skillet. Sprinkle cheese over fillet. Place tomato on top of cheese. Set aside.

1 oz. mushrooms

Wash or brush mushrooms clean. Slice and place on paper plate. Cover with paper towel. Cook **30 seconds (_____) at 100% power.** Set aside.

1 tsp. butter
1 tbsp. chopped fresh or
frozen onion
1 tsp. all-purpose flour
3 tbsp. half and half
1 tbsp. sherry
1/8 tsp. white pepper

Place butter and onion in 1½-pint Menu-ette. Cook **45 seconds (_____) at 100% power.** Add flour, half and half, sherry, pepper, and cooked mushrooms to butter and onion. Mix well. Cook **40 seconds (_____) at 100% power** until mixture boils. Spread mixture on top of fish in Casser-ette. Cook **2 minutes (_____) at 100% power,** giving Casser-ette a half-turn halfway through cooking time. (Autorotating oven: Eliminate turn.) Let stand **1 minute (_____).** Place on plate and serve.

FLOUNDER VERMOUTH

Note: When a recipe calls for cooked or poached fish, use this easy method to guarantee a tender, flavorful product.

3-oz. fresh or frozen flounder or other fillet

If fish is frozen, defrost **1:45 minutes** (_____) **at 30% power.** Rinse off fillet with water and pat dry with paper towel. Place fillet in Casser-ette or Menu-ette Skillet.

1 tbsp. dry vermouth
1/2 tsp. butter
1/8 tsp. salt
1/16 tsp. black pepper
1 tsp. chopped green onion (with top)

Pour vermouth over fillet and dot with butter. Sprinkle with salt, pepper, and green onion. Cover Casser-ette with paper towel. Cook **1 minute (_____)** **at 100% power.** Baste flounder with sauce and replace paper towel. Cook **1 minute (_____) at 100% power.** Let stand **1 minute (_____).** Place on plate and serve.

BREADED FISH STEAK

4-oz. kingfish steak
  or other fish steak

Rinse off fish with water and dry with paper towel. Set aside.

1/2 tbsp. butter

Place butter in custard cup. Cook **20 seconds (_____) at 100% power** until melted. Set aside.

1 tbsp. milk
2 tbsp. dry bread crumbs

Pour milk into shallow bowl. Place bread crumbs on a piece of waxed paper. Dip fish in milk, then in bread crumbs, coating thoroughly.

1/16 tsp. paprika

Place fish in 10" Cooker with Built-in Rack. Pour melted butter over fish and sprinkle with paprika. Cover cooker with paper towel. Cook **1:30 minutes (_____) at 100% power.** Let stand **1 minute (_____).** Place on plate and serve.

SMELTS

4 oz. smelts

Rinse off smelts with water and dry with paper towel. Set aside.

1/4 cup all-purpose flour
1/8 tsp. salt
1/8 tsp. black pepper

Mix flour and spices on paper plate. Dredge smelts in mixture. Leave on plate and set aside.

1/2 cup vegetable oil

Pour oil into 10" browning skillet. Cook **7 minutes (_____) at 100% power.** Place smelts in skillet, largest ones first. Cover skillet with a microwave plastic dome cover. Cook **15 seconds (_____) at 100% power.** Turn smelts over with finger tongs. Cook **45 seconds (_____) at 100% power.** Drain smelts on paper towel. Place on plate and serve.

FRIED SCALLOPS

4 oz. fresh scallops

Rinse off scallops with water and drain on paper towel. Set aside.

1 small egg
1 tsp. vegetable oil
1 tbsp. milk
1/8 tsp. salt
1/8 tsp. black pepper
1 tbsp. all-purpose flour
1/4 cup dry bread crumbs

Place egg, oil, milk, salt, pepper, and flour in small, shallow bowl. Beat vigorously with fork until well mixed. Place bread crumbs on paper plate. Dip scallops in egg mixture, then in bread crumbs. Leave on plate and set aside.

1/4 cup vegetable oil

Pour oil into 8½″ browning skillet. Cook **5 minutes (_____) at 100% power.** Place scallops in skillet and cover with microwave plastic dome cover. Cook **30 seconds (_____) at 100% power.** Turn scallops over with finger tongs. Cook **20 seconds (_____) at 100% power.** Drain on paper towel. Place on small plate and serve.

STEAMED CRABS

4 live crabs
2 tsp. Old Bay Seasoning or other Chesapeake Bay-style seafood seasoning
2 tsp. McCormack Shrimp Boil
1 tsp. salt

Using long tongs, carefully place crabs right side up in 5-quart Corning Ware pot. Sprinkle backs of crabs liberally with spices. Cover pot with lid. Cook **4 minutes (_____) at 100% power** until crabs turn orange. Place on plate and serve.

CRABMEAT THERMIDOR

3 oz. fresh or frozen crabmeat*

If crabmeat is frozen, defrost **5 minutes** (_____) **at 30% power.** Set aside on paper towel.

1 tbsp. butter

Place butter in 1½-pint Menu-ette. Cook **30 seconds** (_____) **at 100% power** until melted.

1 tbsp. all-purpose flour
pinch of salt
1/16 tsp. paprika
1/2 cup milk

Add flour, salt, and paprika to Menu-ette and mix with wire whisk. Add milk and mix with whisk. Cook **1:15 minutes** (_____) **at 100% power** until mixture thickens, stirring once halfway through cooking time.

1/4 tsp. Worcestershire sauce
1/16 tsp. dry mustard
1/16 tsp. Tabasco sauce
1/4 oz. grated cheddar cheese

Add Worcestershire sauce, dry mustard, Tabasco sauce, and cheddar cheese to Menu-ette. Squeeze excess water from crabmeat. Add to Menu-ette and mix well.

1/4 oz. grated cheddar cheese

Sprinkle additional cheese on top. Cook **3 minutes** (_____) **at 50% power,** giving Menu-ette a half-turn halfway through cooking time. (Autorotating oven: Eliminate turn.) Let stand **1 minute** (_____) and serve.

* Frozen crabmeat usually comes in 6-oz. packages. To separate into 3-oz. portions, unwrap package and give crabmeat a sharp rap over the edge of a counter so that it breaks into 2 sections. Rewrap unused portion and put back in freezer.

LOBSTER TAIL

**8-oz. fresh or frozen
lobster tail**

If frozen, defrost lobster tail **4 minutes
(_____) at 30% power.** Cut tail in
half with a strong, sharp knife and remove lobster from shell. Rinse shell
and lobster in water. Pat dry with paper
towel. Place shell halves in 1-quart
Corning Ware pot and place lobster in
shell halves, skin side up. Cook **1:30
minutes (_____) at 100% power.**
Turn lobster over in shell halves and
set aside.

**2 tbsp. butter
1 tbsp. lemon juice
1/16 tsp. Old Bay Seasoning
or other Chesapeake
Bay-style seafood
seasoning
1/16 tsp. salt**

Place butter and lemon juice in custard
cup. Cook **30 seconds (_____) at
100% power** until butter melts. Brush
some lemon butter on lobster. Sprinkle
lobster with spices. Cook **1 minute
(_____) at 100% power.** Let stand
1 minute (_____). Place on plate
and serve with remaining lemon butter.

* The weight of the lobster should not change after defrosting, but some inferior
brands are packed with a lot of water before freezing. If the lobster weighs 3–4
ounces less after thawing, decrease the cooking time.

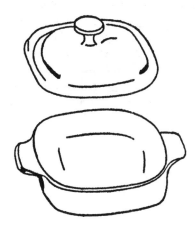

LOBSTER THERMIDOR

8 oz. fresh or frozen small lobster tails

If frozen, defrost lobster **5 minutes** (_____) **at 30% power.** Peel lobster and discard shells. Rinse off lobster with water and drain on paper towel. Cut lobster into 1-inch pieces and set aside.

2 oz. mushrooms

Brush or wash mushrooms clean and drain on paper towel. Slice and spread out on paper plate. Cover plate with paper towel. Cook **45 seconds** (_____) **at 100% power.** Set aside.

1 tbsp. butter
1/16 tsp. salt
1/16 tsp. cayenne pepper
2 tbsp. dry sherry

Heat 6" browning skillet **1 minute** (_____) **at 100% power.** Place butter and lobster in skillet and cover skillet with paper towel. Cook **1 minute** (_____) **at 100% power.** Add mushrooms, salt, cayenne pepper, and sherry. Cook **30 seconds** (_____) **at 100% power.**

1/3 cup heavy cream
1 small egg yolk
1 tsp. grated Parmesan cheese

Put cream and egg yolk into custard cup. Mix with small wire whisk and pour into skillet. Cook **1:20 minutes** (_____) **at 100% power,** stirring 3 times during cooking time. Sprinkle with cheese. Cook **30 seconds** (_____) **at 100% power.** Let stand **1 minute** (_____). Place in small bowl or fancy ramekin and serve.

SPICED STEAMED SHRIMP

Note: When a recipe calls for cooked shrimp, use this easy method, and your shrimp will have added flavor.

4 oz. large fresh shrimp in shells
1/4 tsp. Old Bay Seasoning or other Chesapeake Bay-style seafood seasoning
1/8 tsp. salt

Put shrimp in strainer and rinse off with water. Arrange on paper plate with tails in center. Sprinkle shrimp liberally with spices. Cover with paper towel. Cook **1 minute (_____) at 100% power.** Turn plate halfway around. Cook **30 seconds (_____) at 100% power.** (Autorotating oven: Eliminate turn.) Serve shrimp when cool enough to handle, removing shells and veins before eating.

Variation: Rock shrimp, an inexpensive hardshell shrimp, is simple to cook prepared this way. Cut through back of shell and meat with a small serrated knife, leaving undershell intact. Spread flat and devein, leaving meat in shells. Rinse off with water and drain on paper towel. Arrange open on paper plate, sprinkle with spices, and cover with paper towel. Cook **1 minute (_____) at 100% power.** Serve in shells.

SHRIMP ON CHEESE

4 oz. large fresh shrimp

Peel shrimp and cut each in half lengthwise. Devein and rinse off shrimp with water. Place on paper towel to dry.

1½ tsp. cream cheese
1/2 tsp. Roquefort cheese
1 tsp. minced pimento

Mix cheeses and pimento in Petite Pan and spread evenly over bottom of pan. Place shrimp on top of cheese mixture. Cover pan with lid. Cook **1:15 minutes (_____) at 100% power.** Let stand **1 minute (_____).** Serve in pan.

BAKED SHRIMP

4 oz. large shrimp

Peel shrimp and cut each in half lengthwise. Devein and rinse off shrimp with water. Place on paper towel to dry.

2 tbsp. butter

Place butter in Menu-ette Skillet. Cook **25 seconds (_____) at 100% power** until melted.

1/2 tsp. dry white wine
1/4 tsp. dried basil
1/2 tsp. dried parsley or
  1½ tsp. minced fresh
  or frozen parsley
3/4 tsp. lemon juice
1/8 tsp. minced fresh or
  frozen garlic
1/8 tsp. Worcestershire
  sauce
1/8 tsp. Tabasco sauce
1/16 tsp. salt

Add all remaining ingredients except bread crumbs to skillet and mix well with rubber spatula. Reserve 1 tsp. mixture in custard cup and set aside. Roll shrimp halves one at a time in mixture in skillet and place on one side of skillet. (You may have to tilt skillet so that butter mixture collects on one side, making it easier to coat shrimp.) When all shrimp are coated, arrange them in skillet with tails in center.

1 tbsp. dry bread crumbs

Add bread crumbs to liquid reserved in custard cup and mix well. Sprinkle mixture over shrimp. Cook **1 minute (_____) at 100% power.** Turn skillet halfway around. Cook **45 seconds (_____) at 100% power.** (Autorotating oven: Eliminate turn.) Let stand **1 minute (_____).** Place in small bowl and serve.

MOMMA'S FRIED SHRIMP

**4 oz. jumbo shrimp
(any size will do, but
the larger the better)**

Peel shrimp and slit each down the back three-quarters of the way through. Flatten into butterfly shape and devein. Rinse off shrimp with water and place on paper towel to drain.

**1 small egg
1 tsp. vegetable oil
1 tbsp. all-purpose flour
1 tbsp. milk
1/8 tsp. salt
1/8 tsp. black pepper
2 tbsp. dry bread crumbs**

Place egg, oil, flour, milk, and spices in small bowl. Mix well with fork and set aside. Place bread crumbs on paper plate. Dip shrimp into egg mixture, then into bread crumbs. Leave on plate and set aside.

1/4 cup vegetable oil

Pour oil into 8½" browning skillet. Cook **5:30 minutes (_____) at 100% power.** Place shrimp in oil and cover with microwave plastic dome cover. Cook **15 seconds (_____) at 100% power.** Turn shrimp over with finger tongs. Cook **45 seconds (_____) at 100% power.** Drain on paper towel. Place shrimp on small plate and serve.

 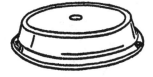

STUFFED SHRIMP

Note: This dish is great to serve to guests. Tripling the recipe (12 shrimp) will fill a dinner plate before cooking. When cooked, the shrimp coil around the stuffing and create a perfect ring of pink shrimp on the plate. Cooking time is **3:30 minutes (_____) at 100% power.**

4 oz. large shrimp

Peel shrimp and slit each down the back three-quarters of the way through. Flatten into butterfly shape and devein. Rinse off with water and place on paper towel to drain.

2 tsp. butter
1 tbsp. chopped fresh or frozen onion
1/3 cup fresh bread crumbs* (grate 3/4 oz. piece of bread)
1/4 tsp. dried parsley or 3/4 tsp. minced fresh or frozen parsley
1/16 tsp. salt
pinch of tarragon

Put butter and onion into Menu-ette Skillet. Cook **45 seconds (_____) at 100% power.** Add remaining ingredients to skillet. Mix well with rubber spatula. Arrange shrimp on paper plate with tails in center. Spread bread crumb mixture evenly over shrimp, covering them completely. Cover plate with paper towel. Cook **1:30 minutes (_____) at 100% power,** giving plate a half-turn halfway through cooking time. (Autorotating oven: Eliminate turn.) Place shrimp in emptied skillet and serve.

* White bread is acceptable, but whole-wheat bread adds extra flavor to the stuffing.

CHEESE-STUFFED SHRIMP

4 oz. large shrimp
1/4 tsp. Old Bay Seasoning
   or other Chesapeake
   Bay-style seafood
   seasoning
1/8 tsp. salt

Rinse off shrimp with water. Arrange on paper plate with tails in center. Sprinkle shrimp with spices. Cook **1 minute** (_____) **at 100% power.** Turn plate halfway around. Cook **30 seconds** (_____) **at 100% power.** Shell and devein shrimp. Put into refrigerator to chill.

2 tsp. Roquefort or blue
   cheese
1 tbsp. cream cheese
1/8 tsp. onion juice*
1/8 tsp. mustard
pinch of rosemary
1/8 tsp. horseradish
2 tsp. dried parsley or
   2 tbsp. minced fresh or
   frozen parsley

Mix cheeses, onion juice, mustard, rosemary, and horseradish thoroughly in small bowl. Slit each shrimp down the back three-quarters of the way through. Stuff cheese mixture into slit in each shrimp. Sprinkle parsley over cheese mixture in each shrimp. Chill before serving.

* To make onion juice, put 1 tsp. fresh or frozen chopped onion into garlic press and squeeze.

SHRIMP IN A BAG

4 oz. medium or large shrimp

Shell shrimp, then cut in half lengthwise. Devein and rinse off shrimp with water. Place on paper towel to dry.

1 tbsp. chopped fresh or frozen onion
1 oz. frozen chopped carrots or thinly sliced fresh carrot
1/8 tsp. minced fresh or frozen garlic or 1/16 tsp. garlic powder
1/8 tsp. salt
1 tsp. butter
1 oz. snow peas, thinly sliced radishes, water chestnuts, celery, or cucumber (choose one)

Put remaining ingredients into 24-oz. cooking bag. Hold bag closed and shake well to mix contents. Place shrimp in bag and shake to mix. Gather bag together about 3 inches down from open end of bag and loosely bind with an elastic or transparent plastic tie. (Do not use a plastic-coated wire tie. If using an electric bag sealer, make a small hole near top of sealed bag.)

With bound end on top, place bag on paper plate. Poke finger through the opening to ensure an unobstructed vent for escaping moisture. Cook **1:45 minutes (_____) at 100% power.** Let stand **1 minute (_____).** Empty contents of bag into small bowl and serve.

SHRIMP EGG FOO YUNG

1/2 oz. mushrooms, cut into 1/2-inch pieces

Place mushrooms on half of a paper towel and cover with other half. Cook **15 seconds (_____) at 100% power.** Set aside.

1/2 oz. bean sprouts

Rinse bean sprouts in small bowl of water, discarding any husks that float to the surface. Drain on paper towel and set aside.

2 oz. shrimp 1 tsp. vegetable oil	Peel and devein shrimp. Rinse off with water and chop into 1/4-inch pieces. Place in 6" browning skillet. Add oil to skillet. Cook **30 seconds (_____)** **at 100% power.** Stir. Cook **15 seconds (_____) at 100% power.** With rubber scraper, empty contents into small strainer placed over 1-cup liquid measure. Set strainer aside.
1 small egg	Beat egg with wire whisk in small bowl until well mixed. Add mushrooms, bean sprouts, and shrimp. Set aside.
3 tbsp. chicken stock (see recipe) or 3 tbsp. water with 1/4 tsp. chicken bouillon granules 1/2 tsp. soy sauce pinch of salt	Add chicken stock, soy sauce, and salt to liquid measure. Cook **45 seconds (_____) at 100% power.**
1 tsp. water 1/2 tsp. cornstarch	Mix water and cornstarch in custard cup and stir into liquid measure. Set aside.
1 tsp. vegetable oil	Pour oil into emptied skillet. Cook **45 seconds (_____) at 100% power.** Pour egg mixture into skillet. Cook **45 seconds (_____) at 100% power.** Loosen egg with turner and flip it over. Set aside.
	Stir sauce in liquid measure. Cook **45 seconds (_____) at 100% power.** Place egg on plate, cover with sauce, and serve.

COQUILLES ST. JACQUES

1 tbsp. butter
1/4 cup dry bread crumbs

Place butter in custard cup. Cook **20 seconds** (_____) **at 100% power** until melted. Add bread crumbs. Mix well and set aside.

1¼ oz. diced Gruyere cheese
1/4 cup mayonnaise
1 tbsp. dry white wine
1/4 tsp. dried parsley or 1 tsp. minced fresh or frozen parsley

Thoroughly mix cheese, mayonnaise, wine, and parsley in small bowl. Set aside.

4 oz. fresh or frozen scallops

Thaw scallops if frozen. If large, cut into 1-inch pieces. Set aside.

1½ tsp. butter

Place butter in Menu-ette Skillet. Cook **20 seconds** (_____) **at 100% power** until melted. Add scallops. Cover skillet with paper towel. Cook **45 seconds** (_____) **at 100% power.** Remove scallops with slotted spoon and place in custard cup.

2 oz. mushrooms
2 tbsp. chopped fresh or frozen onion
2 tsp. dry bread crumbs

Wash or brush mushrooms clean. Slice and add to skillet along with onion. Cook **2 minutes** (_____) **at 100% power.** Add cheese mixture and scallops to skillet and mix. Pour into fancy ramekin or Casser-ette. Top with bread crumbs. Cook **2 minutes** (_____) **at 100% power,** giving dish a half-turn halfway through cooking time. Let stand **1 minute** (_____) and serve.

TRACY'S FAVORITE SEAFOOD MUFFIN

half an English muffin

Toast muffin. Place on plate and set aside.

2 oz. fresh or frozen crabmeat

If crabmeat is frozen, place on plate. Defrost **1 minute (_____) at 30% power.** Squeeze out water and place on paper towel. Wipe plate dry with second paper towel and put crabmeat back on plate.

1 oz. fresh or frozen scallops
1 oz. fresh or frozen shelled and deveined shrimp
1/8 tsp. Old Bay Seasoning or other Chesapeake Bay-style seafood seasoning

Rinse off scallops and shrimp with water. Place on plate and sprinkle with seasoning over all. Cook **40 seconds (_____) at 100% power.** Drain seafood on paper towel.

1/2 tbsp. butter
1/16 tsp. minced fresh or frozen garlic
1/2 tsp. all-purpose flour
1/4 cup half and half

Put butter and garlic into 1½-pint Menu-ette. Cook **25 seconds (_____) at 100% power.** Add flour to Menu-ette and mix with wire whisk. Add half and half and mix with whisk until smooth. Cook **30 seconds (_____) at 100% power** until mixture boils.

2 oz. shredded cheddar cheese
pinch of white pepper
few grains of nutmeg
1 tbsp. Chablis or other dry white wine

Add cheese, pepper, nutmeg, and wine. Mix with whisk, then add drained seafood and cover with lid. Cook **2 minutes (_____) at 30% power.** Stir and set aside.

1/2 cup water

Pour water into 1-pint Menu-ette. Cook **1:15 minutes (_____) at 100% power** until water boils.

(Continued on page 142)

butter
1 extra-large egg

Butter custard cup and break egg into it. Puncture egg yolk with fork. Place cup in water in Menu-ette and cover Menu-ette with lid. Cook **45 seconds (_____) at 100% power.** Set aside. Return cheese sauce to oven. Cook **30 seconds (_____) at 100% power.** While sauce heats, turn egg out of custard cup onto toasted muffin. Using slotted spoon, top egg with seafood and small amount of cheese sauce. Serve muffin with remaining sauce on the side.

BEEF

CHILI

1/2 tsp. vegetable oil
1/4 tsp. minced fresh or
frozen garlic
2 tbsp. (2/3 oz.) chopped
fresh or frozen onion
1½ tbsp. (1/2 oz.) diced
fresh or frozen green
pepper
4 oz. lean ground beef

Place oil, garlic, onion, and green pepper in Gravy Maker Pot. Cook **2 minutes (_____) at 100% power.** add ground beef to pot and mix. Cook **1:30 minutes (_____) at 100% power.** Break up ground beef with fork.

4-oz. tomato
1/8 tsp. ground cumin
3/4 tsp. salt
1 tsp. chili powder
dash of cayenne pepper
3 tbsp. water
8-oz. can kidney beans

Cut tomato into 1/2-inch cubes and add to pot. Add spices, water, and the liquid from the can of beans. Mix well with rubber spatula. Cover pot with lid. Cook **12:30 minutes (_____) at 50% power.** Add beans and mix. Cook **12:30 minutes (_____) at 50% power.** Let stand **10 minutes (_____).** Pour into soup bowl and serve.

GROUND BEEF GOULASH

1/3 cup water
1/2 beef bouillon cube

Place water and bouillon cube in 1-cup liquid measure. Cook **45 seconds** (_____) **at 100% power.** Set aside.

4 oz. lean ground beef
1/2 tsp. vegetable
  shortening or lard
2 tbsp. (2/3 oz.) chopped
  fresh or frozen onion
1/8 tsp. minced fresh or
  frozen garlic

Put ground beef, shortening, onion, and garlic into Gravy Maker Pot and mix with fork. Cook **2 minutes** (_____) **at 100% power.** Mix well, breaking up beef with fork. Cook **30 seconds** (_____) **at 100% power.** Add bouillon mixture to pot.

1 tsp. unfrozen or frozen
  tomato paste
1½ tbsp. (1/2 oz.)
  chopped fresh or frozen
  green pepper
3 oz. minced tomato
2-oz. baking potato, cut
  into 1/2-inch cubes
1/2 tsp. paprika
1/8 tsp. marjoram
1/8 tsp. caraway seeds
1/8 tsp. black pepper
1/8 tsp. salt

Add remaining ingredients and mix well. Cover pot with lid. Cook **15 minutes** (_____) **at 50% power.** Stir. Let stand **5 minutes** (_____). Pour into soup bowl and serve.

GROUND BEEF DRAMBUIE

1/2 tsp. olive or vegetable oil
4 oz. lean ground beef
1/16 tsp. garlic salt
1½ tsp. all-purpose flour

Put oil, ground beef, garlic salt, and flour into Gravy Maker Pot and mix well with fork. Cook **1 minute** (_____) at **100% power**. Stir well. Cook **30 seconds** (_____) at **100% power**.

1 tbsp. Drambuie liqueur
1/8 tsp. salt
1/8 tsp. black pepper
3 tbsp. (3 oz.) tomato sauce
egg noodles (see recipe)*

Add Drambuie, salt, and pepper and mix thoroughly. Add tomato sauce and stir. Cook **2 minutes** (_____) at **50% power**. Stir again. Cover pot with lid. Cook **3 minutes** (_____) at **50% power**. Serve over drained egg noodles.

* Prepare egg noodles before preparing this recipe and let noodles stand in their cooking water while Ground Beef Drambuie is cooking. Drain noodles well before serving.

BEEF AND BEANS

1 slice bacon
4 oz. lean ground beef
1 tbsp. (1/3 oz.) chopped fresh or frozen onion
1 tbsp. (1/3 oz.) chopped fresh or frozen green pepper

Cut bacon into 1/2-inch pieces. Place in Cook 'N' Pour Pan. Cook **1 minute** (_____) at **100% power**. Add ground beef, onion, and green pepper. Mix well. Cook **1 minute** (_____) at **100% power**. Stir. Cook **30 seconds** (_____) at **100% power**.

3 tbsp. (3 oz.) tomato sauce or 3 oz. chopped fresh tomato with 1/8 tsp. salt
8-oz. can pork and beans
1/4 tsp. black pepper

Add tomato sauce, pork and beans, and pepper and stir. Cook **8 minutes** (_____) at **50% power**. (Cooking time may be changed to **4 minutes** (_____) at **100% power**, but ground beef will be less tender.) Stir and cover with lid. Let stand **2 minutes** (_____) and serve.

CORNED BEEF AND CABBAGE

7 oz. cabbage, suey choy, or celery cabbage
1 tsp. butter
1 tsp. brown sugar
dash of salt

Wash cabbage and cut into 1-inch chunks. Put into Menu-ette Skillet. Cover skillet with lid. Cook **5 minutes (_____) at 100% power.** Add butter, sugar, and salt to skillet. Stir and cover skillet with lid. Cook **1 minute (_____) at 100% power.**

3–4-oz. packaged or fresh corned beef (thinly sliced)*

Push cabbage out of the way in skillet. Place beef in skillet and arrange cabbage on top of it. Cover skillet with lid. Cook **2 minutes (_____) at 100% power.** Let stand **1 minute (_____).** Serve in skillet.

* Packaged corned beef is vacuum packed so it keeps well in the refrigerator for a long time. You may find it more practical to keep on hand than fresh meat. However, the freshly sliced corned beef sold in delicatessens cooks just as well in this recipe.

STUFFED CABBAGE

5 oz. cabbage leaves

Rinse cabbage under running water. Shake off excess water and wrap leaves in a double layer of paper towels. Cook **3 minutes (_____) at 100% power.** Spread cabbage leaves out on a 24-inch piece of waxed paper. When cabbage is cool enough to handle, slice off the thick part of each leaf near the stem so leaf will be easier to roll. Set aside.

1/3 cup water
1 tbsp. rice

Pour water into 1½-pint Menu-ette. Cook **1 minute (_____) at 100% power.** Spread rice evenly in Menu-ette. Cook **8 minutes (_____) at 50% power.** Cover Menu-ette with lid and set aside.

3 oz. lean ground beef
2 oz. Italian sausage*
1/4 tsp. salt
1/8 tsp. black pepper
2 tsp. chopped fresh or frozen onion
2 tbsp. (2 oz.) tomato sauce

Place ground beef, Italian sausage, salt, pepper, onion, and tomato sauce in small bowl. Drain rice and add to bowl, mixing thoroughly. Divide stuffing evenly among the spread-out cabbage leaves. Fold the stem end of each leaf over the stuffing, then fold the right and left sides in and roll up the rest of the leaf. Repeat for all leaves. Set rolls aside on waxed paper.

1 tsp. vegetable oil

Heat 8½″ browning skillet **2 minutes (_____) at 100% power.** Pour oil into center of skillet. Place each cabbage roll seam side down in oil, then push roll to outer edge of skillet.

2 oz. cabbage leaves

Wash and thinly slice cabbage. Sprinkle over cabbage rolls. Cook **2 minutes (_____) at 100% power.**

6 tbsp. (6 oz.) tomato sauce (rest of 8-oz. can)
2 tsp. brown sugar
2 tsp. lemon juice

Add remaining ingredients to sauce in can and stir. Pour over cabbage rolls. Cover skillet with lid. Cook **6 minutes (_____) at 100% power,** giving skillet a half-turn halfway through cooking time. (Autorotating oven: Eliminate turn.) Let stand **3 minutes (_____).** Serve in skillet.

* Italian sausage gives the cabbage rolls an added tang, but an extra 2 oz. of beef may be substituted.

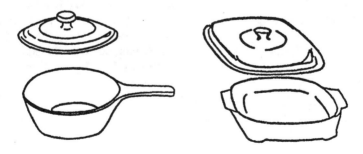

STUFFED GREEN PEPPER

1/3 cup water
1/16 tsp. salt
1 tbsp. long-grain or
　converted rice

Pour water into 1½-pint Menu-ette. Cook **1 minute (_____) at 100% power** until water boils. Add salt and rice. Cover Menu-ette with lid. Cook **8 minutes (_____) at 50% power.** Set aside.

8-oz. green pepper

Slice green pepper through the middle horizontally, creating two pepper cups. Cut stem out of top half (the hole doesn't matter). Clean out and wash both halves. Put the two halves back together and wrap in paper towel. Cook **3 minutes (_____) at 100% power.** Unwrap pepper and place halves cut side up in 1-quart Corning Ware pot. Set aside.

6 oz. lean ground beef
1 tbsp. (1/3 oz.) chopped
　fresh or frozen onion
1 tbsp. ketchup
1/4 tsp. salt
dash of black pepper
1 tbsp. beaten egg

Empty rice into strainer. Put rice, ground beef, onion, ketchup, salt, pepper, and egg into emptied Menu-ette and mix well. Stuff half of mixture into each pepper cup.

2 tbsp. hot water
1/2 cup (4 oz.) tomato sauce
1/2 tsp. all-purpose flour
1/4 tsp. sugar
1/8 tsp. salt
pinch of black pepper

Place remaining ingredients in emptied Menu-ette and mix well. Spread 1 tbsp. sauce over each pepper cup. Cover pot with lid. Cook **3 minutes (_____) at 100% power.** Uncover and pour remaining sauce over pepper cups. Cook **2 minutes (_____) at 100% power.** Cover pot with lid and let stand **2 minutes (_____).** Serve in pot.

MEATLOAF

4 oz. lean ground beef
1/4 cup fresh white or
whole-wheat bread crumbs
(grate 1/2 oz. piece of
bread)
2 tsp. milk
1 tbsp. beaten egg
2 tsp. chopped fresh or
frozen onion
1/2 tsp. Worcestershire sauce
1/8 tsp. salt
dash of black pepper

Mix all ingredients in 1-quart mixing bowl. Pat mixture into 1½-cup loaf-shaped refrigerator dish.* Cook **2:30 minutes** (_____) **at 100% power,** giving dish a half-turn halfway through cooking time. (Autorotating oven: Eliminate turn.) Let stand **3 minutes** (_____). Place on small plate and serve.

* For a drier meatloaf, shape meat into a 1½-inch-high loaf and cook in 10" Cooker with Built-in Rack.

EGGLESS MEATLOAF

4 oz. lean ground beef
4 tsp. crushed saltine
crackers
1 tbsp. ketchup
2 tsp. minced fresh or
frozen green pepper
1 tsp. minced fresh or
frozen onion
1/2 tsp. Worcestershire
sauce
1/16 tsp. salt
1/16 tsp. dried basil

Mix ground beef, crackers, ketchup, green pepper, onion, Worcestershire sauce, and spices in 1-quart mixing bowl. Pat mixture into 1½-cup loaf-shaped refrigerator dish.* Cover dish with paper towel. Cook **2:30 minutes** (_____) **at 100% power,** giving dish a half-turn halfway through cooking time. (Autorotating oven: Eliminate turn.)

1/2 oz. grated cheddar
cheese

Remove paper towel and sprinkle top of meatloaf with cheese. Replace paper towel and let stand 2 minutes (_____) until cheese is melted. Put meatloaf on small plate and serve.

* For a drier meatloaf, shape meat into a 1½-inch-high loaf and cook, uncovered, in 10" Cooker with Built-in Rack. Sprinkle with cheese and cover with a piece of waxed paper. Let stand as above.

GOURMET MEATLOAF

6 oz. lean ground beef
2 tbsp. dry bread crumbs
1½ tbsp. (1/2 oz.) minced
fresh or frozen onion
1/4 tsp. salt
dash of black pepper
1/4 tsp. dried parsley or
1 tsp. minced fresh or
frozen parsley
1 tbsp. beaten egg
2½ tbsp. milk

Mix ground beef, bread crumbs, onion, spices, parsley, egg, and milk in 1-quart mixing bowl. Pat mixture into 1½-cup loaf-shaped refrigerator dish* and set aside.

1/2 tbsp. dark brown sugar
1/4 tsp. dry mustard
1/8 tsp. nutmeg
2 tsp. ketchup

Mix remaining ingredients in emptied bowl. Pour over meatloaf. Cook **2 minutes** (_____) **at 100% power.** Turn dish halfway around. Cook **2 minutes** (_____) **at 50% power.** Let stand **3 minutes** (_____). Place on small plate and serve.

* For a drier meatloaf, shape meat into a 1½-inch-high loaf in 10″ Cooker with Built-in Rack, cover with sauce and cook.

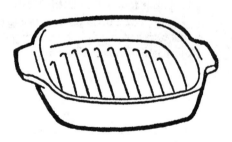

TOMATO SAUCE MEATLOAF

4 oz. lean ground beef
2 tbsp. (2 oz.) tomato sauce
1½ tsp. minced fresh or
 frozen onion
2 tbsp. dry bread crumbs
1/4 tsp. celery seed
1/2 tsp. dried parsley or
 1½ tsp. minced fresh
 or frozen parsley
1 tbsp. beaten egg
1/8 tsp. salt
dash of black pepper
1 tbsp. (1/3 oz.) chopped fresh
 or frozen green pepper
1 tbsp. (1/4 oz.) chopped
 mushrooms

Mix together all ingredients except final tomato sauce in 1-quart mixing bowl. Pat mixture into 1½-cup loaf-shaped refrigerator dish.*

1 tbsp. (1 oz.) tomato sauce

Pour tomato sauce over meatloaf. Cover dish with plastic wrap, puncturing wrap once with fork. Cook **1:30 minutes** (_____) **at 100% power.** Remove plastic wrap and turn dish halfway around. Cook **1:30 minutes** (_____) **at 100% power.** Let stand **2 minutes** (_____). Place on small plate and serve.

* For a drier meatloaf, shape meat into a 1½-inch-high loaf in 10″ Cooker with Built-in Rack and cover with sauce. Cook uncovered.

SWEDISH MEATLOAF

1 tsp. butter
1 tbsp. (1/3 oz.) chopped
fresh or frozen onion

Place butter and onion in Menu-ette Skillet. Cook **1 minute** (_____) at **100% power.**

1½ oz. mushrooms
1/4 cup sour cream

Wash or brush mushrooms clean. Slice and add to skillet. Cook **1:30 minutes** (_____) at **100% power.** Stir in sour cream and set aside.

4 oz. lean ground beef
1/4 cup uncooked oats
1 tbsp. tomato juice
1 tbsp. beaten egg
1/4 tsp. Worcestershire
sauce
1/8 tsp. salt
1/4 tsp. black pepper

Mix remaining ingredients in small bowl. Pat mixture into 16-oz. ceramic souffle dish. Pour mushroom sauce over meatloaf. Cook **3 minutes** (_____) at **100% power,** giving dish a half-turn halfway through cooking time. (Auto-rotating oven: Cook **6 minutes** [_____] at **50% power,** eliminating turn.) Let stand **2 minutes** (_____). Place on small plate and serve.

SALISBURY STEAK AND GRAVY

4 oz. lean ground beef
1/8 tsp. black pepper

Shape ground beef into two 3-inch patties, place on paper plate and set aside. Heat 6″ browning skillet **1:30 minutes** (_____) **at 100% power.** Place patties in skillet and cover skillet with paper towel. Cook **30 seconds** (_____) **at 100% power.** Turn patties over with turner and sprinkle with pepper. Cook **15 seconds** (_____) **at 100% power.** Remove patties to paper plate and set aside.

2 tbsp. (2/3 oz.) chopped
fresh or frozen onion
2 oz. mushrooms

Add onion to skillet. Wash or brush mushrooms clean. Slice and add to skillet. Cook **1:30 minutes** (_____) **at 100% power.**

1/2 cup water
1 tbsp. all-purpose flour
1/8 tsp. salt
1/8 tsp. Kitchen Bouquet

Place remaining ingredients in small jar. Screw lid on jar and shake jar vigorously to mix contents. Pour contents of jar into skillet and stir. Cook **1 minute** (_____) **at 100% power.** Add cooked patties and any liquid in plate and stir. Cover skillet with lid. Cook **1:30 minutes** (_____) **at 50% power.** Let stand **1 minute** (_____). Serve in skillet.

EASY BASIC ROAST

Note: If you choose to serve whipped potatoes as an accompaniment for the following roast recipes, use the water drained from the cooked potatoes for the gravy in place of plain water. It gives the gravy better flavor and, of course, added nutrients.

**1-lb. eye-of-round or
rump roast
1 tsp. Kitchen Bouquet
1/4 tsp. onion salt**

Wipe roast dry with paper towel. Mix Kitchen Bouquet and onion salt in custard cup and brush on roast. Place roast in 1½-quart (7½″ x 6″ x 3¼″) baking dish.

1 slice bacon

Cut bacon in half and place on top of roast. Cover dish with plastic wrap, folding back a corner for venting. Cook **10 minutes (_____) at 50% power.** Set aside plastic wrap and bacon. Turn roast over and cover with bacon. Put plastic wrap back over dish. (Wrap will be loose but will reseal itself during cooking.) Cook **11 minutes (_____) at 50% power.** Place roast on cutting board and cover with plastic wrap.

**1 cup water, stock, or
potato water
1 tbsp. all-purpose flour
1/8 tsp. salt
1/4 tsp. black pepper**

Remove grease from baking dish with Magic Mop or other method. Add remaining ingredients to liquid in dish and mix well with wire whisk. Cook **5 minutes (_____) at 100% power,** stirring after each minute to keep gravy from boiling over. Slice roast thinly and serve with gravy.

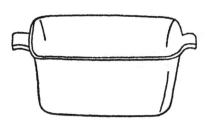

RIB ROAST

1-lb. prime rib roast*
1 small peeled garlic clove
1/2 tsp. coarsely ground
  salt
1 tsp. coarsely ground
  black pepper

Wipe roast dry with paper towel. Cut garlic in half lengthwise. Rub roast with cut sides of garlic. Cut slits in fatty side of roast and insert garlic pieces. Sprinkle roast with salt and pepper and press spices into roast. The roast will be too small to stand up, so lay it on its side in 10" Cooker with Built-in Rack (this pan is best for collecting drippings).

Cover cooker with paper towel. Cook **10 minutes (_____) at 100% power,** giving cooker a quarter-turn after each **2:30 minutes (_____)** of cooking time. Turn roast over halfway through cooking time and replace paper towel over cooker. (Autorotating oven: Cook **5 minutes (_____) at 100% power.** Turn roast over and replace paper towel. Cook another **5 minutes (_____) at 100% power.)** Remove roast, place on cutting board, and cover with paper towel.

1 cup water, stock, or
  potato water
1 tbsp. all-purpose flour
1/8 tsp. salt
1/4 tsp. black pepper
1/4 tsp. Kitchen Bouquet

Drain drippings into an empty cup and set aside. Pour water into cooker. Cook **1 minute (_____) at 100% power** to deglaze. Pour contents of cooker into Gravy Maker Pot, scraping inside with rubber spatula. Add remaining ingredients. Drippings in cup should be settled; pour off and discard grease on top. Remove remaining grease with Magic Mop or other method. Pour drippings into pot and mix well with wire whisk. Cook **5 minutes (_____) at 100% power,** stirring with wire whisk after each minute to keep gravy from

(Continued on page 156)

boiling over. Remove bones and outer layer of fat from roast. Slice roast thinly and serve with gravy.

* When buying a rib roast from the butcher, ask for the small end. Besides being the best part of the roast, the small end has a shape that is ideal for the microwave oven.

ROAST WITH MUSHROOMS

1 oz. mushrooms

Wash or brush mushrooms clean. Slice, place on paper plate, and cover with paper towel. Cook **30 seconds (_____) at 100% power.** Set aside.

1-lb. eye-of-round roast
1/4 tsp. salt
1/4 tsp. black pepper
2 oz. sliced onion

Wipe roast dry with paper towel. Sprinkle with salt and pepper. Arrange onion in 1½-quart (7½" x 6" x 3¼") baking dish and place roast on top. Arrange mushrooms on top of roast. Set aside.

1½ tbsp. sherry
2 tbsp. water
1 tbsp. ketchup
1/8 tsp. minced fresh or frozen garlic
pinch of dry mustard
pinch of marjoram
pinch of rosemary
pinch of thyme

Mix sherry, water, ketchup, garlic, and spices in 1-cup liquid measure. Pour over roast. Cover dish with plastic wrap, folding back a corner for venting. Cook **10 minutes (_____) at 50% power,** giving dish a quarter-turn halfway through cooking time. Remove plastic wrap and mushrooms and set aside. Turn roast over and put mushrooms back on top of roast. Put plastic wrap back on dish. (Wrap will be loose but will reseal itself during cooking.) Cook **10 minutes (_____) at 50% power,** giving dish a quarter-turn halfway through cooking time. (Autorotating oven: Cook **20 minutes (_____) at 50% power,** turning roast over halfway through cooking time and eliminating turns.) Remove roast, place on cutting board, and cover roast with plastic wrap.

1 cup water, stock, or potato water
1 tbsp. all-purpose flour
1/8 tsp. salt
1/4 tsp. black pepper
1/4 tsp. Kitchen Bouquet

Remove grease from liquid in baking dish with Magic Mop or other method. Add remaining ingredients to liquid and stir well with wire whisk until flour dissolves. Cook **5 minutes (_____) at 100% power,** stirring with wire whisk after each minute to keep gravy from boiling over. Slice roast thinly and serve with gravy.

BUTTERMILK POT ROAST

1-lb. chuck roast
1 cup buttermilk

Put a 1-gallon plastic bag into 1½-quart (7½" x 6" x 3¼") baking dish. Place roast in bag. Pour buttermilk over roast. Gather bag tightly around roast and fasten bag with wire twist. Buttermilk should cover roast as completely as possible. Place baking dish in refrigerator overnight. When ready to cook, remove roast from bag, discard buttermilk and bag, and wipe roast dry with paper towel.

1/16 tsp. ground cumin
1/4 tsp. black pepper
1/8 tsp. Tabasco sauce
1/2 tbsp. all-purpose flour

Mix spices and flour in custard cup and rub into roast. Set aside.

1/2 tbsp. vegetable shortening or lard

Place shortening in emptied baking dish. Cook **2 minutes (_____) at 100% power** until melted. Put roast in dish. Cook **3 minutes (_____) at 100% power,** turning roast over halfway through cooking time.

(Continued on page 158)

1 oz. sliced onion
1/4 tsp. salt
1/16 tsp. black pepper
1/4 cup water or stock
1 tbsp. leftover coffee or
   1 tbsp. water with
   1/8 tsp. instant coffee

Place onion under roast. Add remaining ingredients to dish. Cover dish with plastic wrap. Cook **8 minutes (_____) at 50% power,** giving dish a quarter-turn halfway through cooking time. Turn roast over and put plastic wrap back on dish. (Wrap will be loose but will reseal itself during cooking.) Cook **8 minutes (_____) at 50% power,** giving dish a quarter-turn halfway through cooking time. (Autorotating oven: Cook **8 minutes [_____] at 50% power,** eliminating turn. Turn roast over and replace plastic wrap. Cook **8 minutes [_____] at 50% power.)** Let stand **5 minutes (_____).** Place roast on cutting board and cover with plastic wrap.

1 cup water, stock, or
   potato water
1 tbsp. all-purpose flour
1/8 tsp. salt
1/4 tsp. black pepper
1/4 tsp. Kitchen Bouquet

Remove grease from baking dish with Magic Mop or other method. Add remaining ingredients to baking dish and stir well with wire whisk until flour dissolves. Cook **5 minutes (_____) at 100% power,** stirring after each minute to keep gravy from boiling over. Slice roast thinly and serve with gravy.

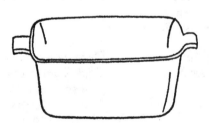

STEAK

1/2 tsp. butter
4 oz. boneless steak
trimmed of fat (filet,
rib, etc.)

Heat 6″ browning skillet* **3 minutes**
(_____) **at 100% power.** Lightly
butter one side of steak and place buttered side down in skillet. Cover skillet
with paper towel. Cook **1:45 minutes**
(_____) **at 100% power.** Discard
paper towel and turn steak over with
finger tongs.

1/16 tsp. salt
1/16 tsp. black pepper

Sprinkle steak with salt and pepper.
Cook **15 seconds** (_____) at **100%**
power until done. Place steak in serving dish.

1/2 tsp. butter

Put butter in skillet and mix with drippings using rubber spatula. Scrape onto
steak and serve.

* When cooking a steak weighing approximately 1 lb., use a Corning Ware
  Browning Griddle; for a steak larger than 1 lb., use a Corning Ware Browning
  Grill, which has a well to hold meat juices.

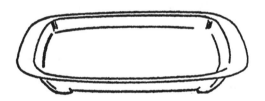

BEEF · 159

STEAK AND MUSHROOMS

2 oz. mushrooms

Wash or brush mushrooms clean. Slice, put on paper plate, and cover with paper towel. Cook **45 seconds** (_____) **at 100% power.** Set aside.

1/2 tsp. butter
4 oz. boneless steak
trimmed of fat

Heat 6″ browning skillet **3 minutes** (_____) **at 100% power.** Butter one side of steak and place buttered side down in skillet. Cover skillet with paper towel. Cook **1:45 minutes** (_____) **at 100% power.** Turn steak over with finger tongs.

1/8 tsp. salt
1/4 tsp. black pepper

Sprinkle steak with salt and pepper. Place mushrooms around steak. Cook **30 seconds** (_____) **at 100% power.** Put steak and mushrooms in small serving dish.

1/2 tsp. butter

Mix butter and drippings with rubber spatula. Scrape onto steak and serve.

STEAK AND ONIONS

2½-oz. onion

Peel and slice onion and place on paper plate. Cover with paper towel. Cook **1:30 minutes** (_____) **at 100% power** until at least one onion tip turns brown. Set aside.

1/2 tsp. butter
4 oz. beef cubed sirloin
   or round minute steak

Heat 6″ browning skillet **3:30 minutes** (_____) **at 100% power.** Butter one side of steak and place buttered side down in skillet. Cover skillet with paper towel. Cook **30 seconds** (_____) **at 100% power.** Remove and discard paper towel. Turn steak over with finger tongs.

1/8 tsp. salt
1/8 tsp. black pepper

Sprinkle steak with salt and pepper. Arrange onion around steak. Cook **45 seconds** (_____) **at 100% power.** Cover with paper towel and let stand **1 minute** (_____). Place steak and onions on small plate and serve.

ITALIAN STEAK

4 oz. beef cubed sirloin or round minute steak
1/4 tsp. olive oil
1/8 tsp. black pepper

Flatten steak with meat pounder. Heat 6″ browning skillet **3:30 minutes (_____) at 100% power.** Spread oil over one side of steak with back of measuring spoon and place oiled side down in skillet. Cover skillet with paper towel. Cook **30 seconds (_____) at 100% power.** Remove and discard paper towel. Turn steak over with finger tongs. Sprinkle with pepper. Cook **15 seconds (_____) at 100% power.** Place steak on plate and set aside.

3 tbsp. (3 oz.) tomato sauce
dash of garlic salt
1/8 tsp. dried basil
1/8 tsp. oregano
1/8 tsp. dried parsley or
1/2 tsp. minced fresh or frozen parsley

Mix tomato sauce, spices, and parsley in skillet. Cover skillet with lid. Cook **2 minutes (_____) at 100% power.** Put steak and any liquid on plate into skillet. Spoon sauce over steak. Cover skillet with lid. Cook **1:30 minutes (_____) at 50% power.** Let stand **2 minutes (_____).** Serve in skillet.

LEFTOVER MEAT STEW

2 oz. carrots, cut into
1/4-inch slices
1/4 cup water
2-oz. baking potato, cut
into 1/2-inch cubes

Put carrots and water into Cook 'N'
Pour Pan. Cover with lid. Cook **2 minutes** (_____) **at 100% power.** Add
potato and replace lid. Cook **3 minutes** (_____) **at 100% power.**

2 oz. cooked meat (steak
left over from a
restaurant meal will do)
1/3 cup water or leftover
gravy
1/2 beef bouillon cube
1/16 tsp. salt
1 tsp. all-purpose flour

Cut meat into 1/2-inch cubes and add
to pan. Add water, bouillon, salt, and
flour to pan and mix well. Replace lid.
Cook **1 minute** (_____) **at 100%
power.**

1 oz. (1/4 cup) fresh or
frozen peas

Stir in peas and replace lid. Cook **1
minute** (_____). Let stand **2 minutes** (_____). Pour into soup bowl
and serve.

OTHER MEATS

VEAL AU JUS

3-oz. slice boneless veal trimmed of fat and gristle
1/4 tsp. vegetable oil or olive oil
1/16 tsp. salt
1/16 tsp. black pepper

Heat 6″ browning skillet **1 minute** (_____) **at 100% power.** Coat top of veal with oil and place oiled side down in skillet. Cook **30 seconds** (_____) **at 100% power.** Turn veal over with finger tongs. Sprinkle with salt and pepper. Cook **20 seconds** (_____) **at 100% power.** Place veal on small plate. Scrape juices in skillet over veal with rubber spatula and serve.

VEAL CUTLETS

Note: When doubling recipe, cook half the veal, then reheat the oil **1:45 minutes (_____) at 100% power** before cooking the other half.

4 oz. sliced boneless veal trimmed of fat and gristle

Pound each slice of veal with meat pounder until paper-thin. Set aside.

1 small egg
1/8 tsp. salt
1/8 tsp. black pepper
2 tbsp. dry bread crumbs
2 tbsp. Italian bread crumbs

Break egg into shallow bowl and add salt and pepper. Mix well with fork. Place bread crumbs on one end of a 24-inch piece of waxed paper. Mix crumbs together. Dip veal slices one at a time into egg mixture, then into bread crumbs. Place coated slices on waxed paper and set aside.

1/2 cup vegetable oil

Pour oil into 10″ browning skillet. Heat **7 minutes (_____) at 100% power.** Arrange veal in skillet and cover with microwave plastic dome cover. Cook **40 seconds (_____) at 100% power.** Turn veal over with finger tongs and replace cover. Cook **30 seconds (_____) at 100% power.** Place veal on paper towel to drain, then place on small plate and serve.

Variation: Veal Cutlets Parmesan

Veal Cutlets (see above)

Cook veal according to recipe and set aside.

1 tsp. olive oil
1 small peeled garlic clove

Put oil and garlic in 1½-pint Menu-ette. Prop up one end with a plastic jar lid so that the oil will collect in one area and cover garlic. Cook **2:30 minutes (_____) at 100% power** until garlic begins to brown. Remove and discard garlic.

8-oz. can tomato sauce
1 tsp. oregano

Add tomato sauce and oregano and mix well. Cover Menu-ette with lid.

2 oz. grated fresh or
frozen Mozzarella cheese

Cook **3:30 minutes** (_____) at **100% power.** Spoon 2 tbsp. tomato mixture into pie plate or onto dinner plate and spread evenly over bottom. Arrange drained veal cutlets on top of sauce. Cover cutlets with cheese. Spoon some of remaining sauce over cheese and spread evenly over each cutlet with rubber spatula. Cook **1:40 minutes** (_____) **at 100% power** until cheese melts. Set aside. Reheat remaining sauce **45 seconds** (_____) **at 100% power** and serve separately with veal. (Plain rice is a good accompaniment for this dish. The extra sauce can be served over the rice.)

LIVER AND BACON

1 tbsp. all-purpose flour
1/8 tsp. salt
1/8 tsp. black pepper
4 oz. calf liver, sliced
  1/4-inch thick

Mix flour and spices on paper plate. Dredge liver in flour mixture. Leave on plate and set aside.

6 slices bacon

Place bacon in 10″ browning skillet. Cover with microwave plastic dome cover or paper towel. Cook **5:30 minutes** (_____) **at 100% power,** rearranging bacon with finger tongs halfway through cooking time for even cooking.

When bacon is cooked, push it to one side with finger tongs and arrange liver in skillet. Cook **1 minute** (_____) **at 100% power.** Turn liver over with tongs. Cook **30 seconds** (_____) **at 100% power.** Drain liver and bacon on paper towel. Place on plate and serve.

BARBECUED BEEF LIVER

Note: This recipe is great for converting liver-haters into liver-lovers. Children usually love liver cooked this way.

2 oz. sliced white onion
1 tsp. butter (optional)

Place onion and butter in Menu-ette Skillet. Cook **3 minutes** (_____) at **100% power.** Set aside.

4 oz. calf liver

Slice liver into 1/4-inch strips, then cut strips into 1-inch pieces. Push onions to outer edge of skillet with rubber spatula. Place liver in center of skillet and cover liver with onions.

1½ tsp. white vinegar
1½ tsp. Worcestershire
sauce
1½ tsp. water
1/16 tsp. black pepper
1/16 tsp. chili powder
1/2 tsp. sugar
1/2 tsp. mustard
2 tbsp. ketchup

Place remaining ingredients in 1-cup liquid measure. Mix thoroughly with small wire whisk and pour over liver and onions. Cover skillet with lid. Cook **4 minutes** (_____) **at 50% power.** Stir mixture with rubber spatula. Cook **30 seconds** (_____) **at 100% power.** Cover with lid and let stand **1 minute** (_____). Serve liver in skillet.

LIVER AND ONIONS

5 oz. sliced white onion

Place onion on paper plate and cover with paper towel. Cook **3 minutes** (_____) **at 100% power** until tip of at least one onion turns brown. Set aside.

1 tbsp. all-purpose flour
1/8 tsp. salt
4 oz. calf liver, sliced 1/4-inch thick

Mix flour and salt on paper plate. Dredge liver in flour mixture. Leave on plate and set aside.

1/3 cup vegetable oil

Pour oil into 8½" browning skillet. Heat **3 minutes** (_____) **at 100% power.** Place liver in skillet and cover skillet with paper towel. Cook **30 seconds** (_____) **at 100% power.** Remove and discard paper towel. Turn liver over with finger tongs and arrange onions around liver. Cook **45 seconds** (_____) **at 100% power.** Drain on paper towel. Place on plate and serve.

LIVER STROGANOFF

4 oz. calf liver

Slice liver into 1/2-inch strips, then cut each strip into 2-inch pieces. Set aside.

1 tbsp. all-purpose flour
1/8 tsp. salt
1/8 tsp. black pepper
1/8 tsp. paprika

Shake flour and spices together in plastic sandwich bag. Put a few pieces of liver into bag and shake until pieces are coated thoroughly. Set pieces aside on paper plate. Repeat for remaining liver.

1 tsp. vegetable oil

Place oil in 6" browning skillet. Heat **45 seconds (_____) at 100% power.** Arrange liver in a single layer in skillet. Cook **30 seconds (_____) at 100% power.** Turn liver pieces over with finger tongs. Cook **30 seconds (_____) at 100% power.**

2 tbsp. white wine
3 tbsp. sour cream
1/2 tsp. dried parsley or
  2 tsp. minced fresh or
  frozen parsley

Put remaining ingredients into custard cup and mix well. Pour over liver. Cook **1 minute (_____) at 100% power.** Cover skillet with lid and let stand **1 minute (_____).** Serve in skillet.

LIVER WITH STUFFING

2 tsp. butter
1 tbsp. chopped fresh or
    frozen onion
1/3 cup fresh bread crumbs
    (grate 3/4 oz. piece of
    bread)
1/8 tsp. salt
dash of black pepper
pinch of thyme
pinch of marjoram

Place butter and onion in Menu-ette Skillet. Cook **45 seconds (_____) at 100% power**. Add bread crumbs and spices to skillet and mix well. Set aside.

4 oz. calf liver, sliced
    1/2-inch thick

Place liver on cutting board. Cut pocket in liver with sharp knife.* Fill pocket with stuffing mixture.

1 tsp. butter
1 slice bacon

Place butter in emptied skillet. Pick up liver with slotted turner and place on top of butter. Place bacon on top of liver. Cover skillet with paper towel. Cook **1:45 minutes (_____) at 100% power** until liver is cooked. If you prefer crispy bacon, remove bacon from liver and fold it up in paper towel. Cook **30 seconds (_____) at 100% power** until crisp. Put bacon back on top of liver. Place liver on plate with turner and serve.

* If liver is already sliced 1/4-inch thick and is in one piece, fold it in half to create a pocket for the stuffing. If liver is sliced 1/4-inch thick and is in two pieces, cover one piece with stuffing and cover stuffing with second piece.

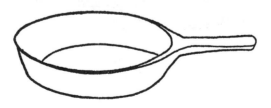

LAMB PATTIE

4½ oz. lean ground lamb
1/4 tsp. dried parsley or
   1/2 tsp. minced fresh or
   frozen parsley
1/8 tsp. salt
1/8 tsp. black pepper

Combine lamb and parsley in small bowl. Shape into 5-inch pattie and set aside. Heat 6" browning skillet **2:45 minutes (_____) at 100% power.** Place lamb pattie in skillet and cover skillet with paper towel. Cook **40 seconds (_____) at 100% power.** Turn pattie over with turner. Sprinkle with salt and pepper. Cook **1 minute (_____) at 100% power.** Let stand **1 minute (_____).** Place on plate and serve.

Variation: Add 1/8 tsp. curry powder when adding salt and pepper.

LAMB CHOP

6 oz. lamb chop (1 large or
   2 small chops)
1/8 tsp. salt
1/16 tsp. black pepper

Heat 6" browning skillet **3:30 minutes (_____) at 100% power.** Place lamb chop in skillet and cover skillet with paper towel. Cook **2 minutes (_____) at 100% power.** Turn chop over with finger tongs. Sprinkle with salt and pepper. Cook **1:15 minutes (_____) at 100% power.** Let stand **1 minute (_____).** Place on small plate and serve.

MOMMA'S BREAST OF LAMB

1/2 cup water
4 tsp. rice

Pour water into 1½-pint Menu-ette. Cook **1 minute** (_____) **at 100% power.** Add rice. Cook **8 minutes** (_____) **at 50% power.** Cover Menu-ette with lid and set aside.

1 lb. breast of lamb
1/4 tsp. salt
1/4 tsp. black pepper

Wipe lamb dry with paper towel. Cut a lengthwise slit in lamb with sharp knife to form a pocket. Rub inside of lamb pocket with salt and pepper. If there is any meat hanging off one corner of breast, cut it off, mince with knife, and place in small bowl. Drain rice in strainer and add to bowl.

1 small egg
1/4 cup grated Romano cheese
1 tbsp. dried parsley or
  1/4 cup minced fresh or
  frozen parsley
1/4 cup fresh bread
  crumbs (grate 1/2 oz.
  piece of bread)

Add remaining ingredients to bowl and mix well. Spoon mixture into pocket. Close slit with toothpicks or sew it closed with large needle and thick thread. Place lamb in 10″ Cooker with Built-in Rack and cover cooker with paper towel. Cook **13 minutes** (_____) at **100% power.** Let stand **2 minutes** (_____). Slice, place on small plate, and serve.

PAN-BROILED PORK CHOP

10-oz. center cut pork chop,
  1 inch thick (a thinner
  chop will be less tender)
1/16 tsp. salt
1/8 tsp. black pepper

Heat 6″ browning skillet **3 minutes** (_____) at **100% power.** Place chop in skillet and cover with lid. Cook **2:45 minutes** (_____) **at 100% power.** Remove lid and turn chop over with finger tongs. Sprinkle chop with salt and pepper. Replace lid. Cook **5 minutes** (_____) **at 100% power.** Let stand **2 minutes** (_____). Place on small plate and and serve.

TENDER PORK CHOP

4 oz. butterfly pork chop, fat removed

Cut chop in half. Flatten each piece with meat pounder. Set aside.

2 tbsp. vegetable oil

Pour oil into 6" browning skillet. Heat **2:30 minutes (_____) at 100% power.** Place pork in skillet and cover skillet with paper towel. Cook **45 seconds (_____) at 100% power.** Remove paper towel and set aside.

1/16 tsp. salt
1/8 tsp. black pepper

Turn pork over with finger tongs and sprinkle with salt and pepper. Cook **45 seconds (_____) at 100% power.** Drain pork on paper towel for **2 minutes (_____).** Place on small plate and serve.

SPANISH PORK CHOP

4 oz. butterfly pork chop
1/8 tsp. salt
1/16 tsp. black pepper
1 oz. thinly sliced onion
1 tbsp. ketchup

Place chop in Casser-ette. Sprinkle with salt and pepper and cover completely with onion slices. Spread ketchup over onion, but do not go beyond edge of chop. Set aside.

1/4 cup white vinegar
1/4 cup water

Mix vinegar and water in 1-cup liquid measure. Carefully pour mixture around chop until liquid is just below top edge of chop. Cover with microwave plastic dome cover. Cook **4 minutes (_____) at 100% power,** giving Casser-ette a half-turn halfway through cooking time. (Autorotating oven: Eliminate turn.) Remove chop and topping with slotted turner and place on small plate. Let stand **2 minutes (_____)** and serve.

BREADED PORK CHOP

1 small egg
1½ tsp. milk
1 tbsp. lime juice
1/2 tsp. salt
1/2 tsp. salad herb spices
1/8 tsp. black pepper
1/8 tsp. garlic salt

Mix egg, milk, lime juice, and spices in small, shallow bowl. Beat with small fork until well mixed.

2 tbsp. corn flake crumbs
4 oz. butterfly pork chop

Place crumbs on a piece of waxed paper. Dip chop into egg mixture, then into crumbs. Place chop in Casser-ette. Cook **5 minutes (_____) at 50% power,** turning chop over with finger tongs halfway through cooking time. Let stand **2 minutes (_____).** Place on small plate and serve.

PORK MINUTE STEAK

1 small egg
1/16 tsp. salt
1/16 tsp. black pepper

Mix egg, salt, and pepper in shallow bowl and set aside.

3 tbsp. dry bread crumbs

Place bread crumbs on paper plate and set aside.

4-oz. pork minute steak

If steak is more than 1/4 inch thick, flatten with a meat pounder. Coat steak well with egg mixture, then dredge in bread crumbs. Set aside on paper plate.

2 tbsp. vegetable oil

Pour oil into 6″ browning skillet. Heat **3 minutes (_____) at 100% power.** Place steak in skillet and cover skillet with paper towel. Cook **40 seconds (_____) at 100% power.** Discard paper towel and turn steak over with turner. Cook **40 seconds (_____) at 100% power.** Place steak on small plate. Let stand **2 minutes (_____)** and serve.

BARBECUED PORK RIBS

8 oz. pork loin back ribs

Wipe ribs clean with paper towel. Cut ribs into individual sections so that each has a bone. Set aside.

1/4 tsp. dried basil
1/4 tsp. cumin
1/4 tsp. chili powder

Crush spices together in mortar and pestle or mix in custard cup. Dip one rib into spices and use it as a brush to spread spices on other ribs. Arrange seasoned ribs on their sides in center of 10″ Cooker with Built-in Rack. Cover cooker with a piece of waxed paper. Cook **1:15 minutes (_____) at 100% power,** then cook **3 minutes (_____) at 50% power.** Turn ribs over and rearrange. Replace waxed paper. Cook **6 minutes (_____) at 50% power.**

your choice of barbecue sauce (see recipes)

Prepare barbecue sauce according to directions. Pick up each rib with finger tongs, dip in sauce to coat, then place in Casser-ette. Pour remaining sauce over all. Cook **2:30 minutes (_____) at 50% power.** Let stand **2 minutes (_____)** and serve.

PORK IN A BAG

3 tbsp. (1 oz.) chopped
   fresh or frozen onion
4-oz. baking potato

4 oz. pork tenderloin*
1/2 tsp. Kitchen Bouquet
1/2 cup fresh or frozen
   peas (1/2 lb. unshelled
   fresh)

2/3 cup water
1 tsp. all-purpose flour
1/8 tsp. salt
1/8 tsp. black pepper
1/2 tsp. beef bouillon
   granules or 1/2 beef
   bouillon cube

Place onion in 24-oz. cooking bag. Peel and wash potato. Cut into 1/4-inch slices and cut larger slices in half. Add to bag.

Cut pork into 1/2-inch-thick slices, then cut each slice in half. Place pork in custard cup. Add Kitchen Bouquet and mix until all pieces are thoroughly coated. Add pork and peas to bag.

Put remaining ingredients in 1-cup liquid measure. Mix well with wire whisk and pour mixture into bag. Seal bag with electric sealer or close with transparent plastic tie. Place bag in Gravy Maker Pot or Cook 'N' Pour Pan. Make a small hole in upper part of electrically sealed bag to allow moisture to escape. Cook **15 minutes (_____) at 50% power.** Let stand **3 minutes (_____).** Empty bag into soup bowl and serve.

* Frozen pork tenderloin slices easily with a large, sturdy knife. Cooking time remains the same.

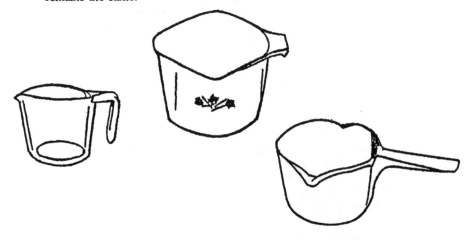

PORK ROAST

Note: This dish is delicious served with applesauce. Use leftover roast for a variation on the Barbecue Beef Sandwich or in Egg-Fried Rice (see recipes).

1-lb. center-cut boneless pork loin roast
1 small peeled garlic clove

Wipe roast dry with paper towel. Cut garlic in half and rub roast with cut sides. Discard garlic.

1/2 tsp. coarsely ground salt
1/2 tsp. black pepper

Sprinkle roast with salt and pepper and press spices into roast. Place in 10″ Cooker with Built-in Rack and cover cooker with paper towel. Cook **15 minutes** (_____) **at 50% power.** Turn cooker halfway around and turn roast over. Replace paper towel. Cook **15 minutes** (_____) **at 50% power.** Let stand **5 minutes** (_____). Slice thinly, place on small plate, and serve.

HAM SLICE

11-oz. slice cooked ham*
1/2 tsp. butter

Heat browning grill **4 minutes** (_____) **at 100% power.** Trim fat from ham and spread butter on one side. Place ham buttered side down on grill. Cook **2 minutes** (_____) **at 100% power.** Turn ham over with finger tongs. Cook **30 seconds** (_____) **at 100% power.** Let stand **30 seconds** (_____). Place on small plate and serve.

* This is usually the smallest slice of ham available in supermarkets. Leftover slices may be used in Ham and Eggs or Ham and Cheese Sandwich (see recipes).

HUNGARIAN BACON AND TOMATOES

4 oz. bacon

Cut bacon into 2-inch pieces. Put two paper towels on paper plate. Arrange bacon on paper towels and cover with another paper towel. Cook **4 minutes (_____) at 100% power** until bacon is crisp. Drain bacon on top paper towel.

8-oz. can stewed tomatoes
1/4 tsp. paprika

Empty tomatoes into 1½-pint Menu-ette and add paprika. Stir well and cover with lid. Cook **2 minutes (_____) at 100% power.** Add drained bacon. Mix well and cover with lid. Cook **2 minutes (_____) at 100% power.** Let stand **1 minute (_____).** Pour into soup bowl and serve.

PEPPERS, ONIONS, AND SAUSAGE

6 oz. fresh green pepper

Wash pepper. Remove and discard core and seeds. Slice pepper and place on paper plate. Cover plate with paper towel. Cook **3:30 minutes (_____) at 100% power.** Set aside.

6 oz. onion

Peel and slice onion. Place on paper plate and cover with paper towel. Cook **2 minutes (_____) at 100% power** until tip of at least one slice turns brown. Set aside.

4 oz. Italian sausage

Cut sausage into 4-inch links. Puncture several, holes in each link with fork. Place in 8½" browning skillet. Cook **1:30 minutes (_____) at 100% power.** Turn links over with finger tongs. Cook **1:15 minutes (_____) at 100% power.** Push sausage to center of skillet and surround with cooked peppers and onions. Cover skillet with lid. Cook **2 minutes (_____) at 50% power.** Let stand **1 minute (_____)** and serve in skillet.

SAUSAGE STROGANOFF

1½ cups water
1/8 tsp. salt
1/8 tsp. vegetable oil
2 oz. (about 1 cup) egg
   noodles

Pour water into 1½-quart Corning Ware pot. Cook **3:15 minutes** (_____) **at 100% power** until water boils. Add salt and oil and stir. Add noodles, spreading them out evenly in pot. Cook **4 minutes** (_____) **at 100% power.** Stir. Cover pot with lid and set aside.

3 oz. Italian sausage

Remove and discard sausage casing. Put sausage into Gravy Maker Pot or Cook 'N' Pour Pan. Break up sausage into small pieces with small fork. Cook **1 minute** (_____) **at 100% power.** Stir with fork. Cook **30 seconds** (_____) **at 100% power.** Remove sausage with slotted spoon and drain on paper towel.

1½ tsp. chopped fresh or
   frozen onion
1½ oz. chopped mushrooms

Place onion and mushrooms in Gravy Maker Pot. Cook **45 seconds** (_____) **at 100% power.** Remove onion and mushrooms with slotted spoon and drain on paper towel. Wipe pot clean with another paper towel.

1 tsp. all-purpose flour
2 tbsp. sour cream
2 tbsp. milk
1/4 tsp. Worcestershire
   sauce
1/8 tsp. soy sauce
1/16 tsp. paprika

Put remaining ingredients into pot and mix with wire whisk. Add sausage, onion, and mushrooms and mix well. Cover pot with lid. Cook **2 minutes** (_____) **at 50% power.** Stir and replace lid. Cook **1 minute** (_____) **at 50% power.** Let stand **1 minute** (_____). Drain noodles and place on plate. Top with stroganoff and serve.

BEANS AND FRANKS

3 oz. frankfurters
1 tsp. butter
1 oz. (2 tbsp.) chopped fresh or frozen onion

Cut frankfurters diagonally into 1/4-inch pieces. Place butter, onion, and frankfurters in 6″ browning skillet. Cook **1 minute (_____) at 100% power.** Turn frankfurter slices over with finger tongs. Cook **1 minute (_____) at 100% power.**

8-oz. can pork and beans
1 tsp. mustard

Add remaining ingredients to mixture. Mix well and cover skillet with lid. Cook **3 minutes (_____) at 100% power.** Mix well and replace lid. Let stand **1 minute (_____).** Serve in skillet.

CHEESE AND FRANKS

2 slices bacon

Put paper towel on paper plate. Place bacon on top and cover with another paper towel. Cook **1 minute (_____) at 100% power** until bacon is partially cooked. Set aside.

2 frankfurters (4 oz.)
1 slice American cheese

Cut slit in each frankfurter lengthwise. Do not cut all the way through. Fold cheese in half and break into two pieces. Fold each piece in half lengthwise and insert one folded piece of cheese in each frankfurter slit. Wrap one bacon slice barber-pole style around each frankfurter. Place cheese side up in Menuette Skillet. **Cook 1 minute (_____) at 100% power** until cheese melts. **Let stand 1 minute (_____).** Place on plate and serve.

POULTRY

CHICKEN WITH MUSHROOMS

1 oz. mushrooms

Wash or brush mushrooms clean. Chop and place on paper plate. Cover with paper towel. Cook **1 minute (_____) at 100% power.**

1/4 cup buttermilk or sour milk*
2 tsp. all-purpose flour
1 tbsp. (1/3 oz.) chopped celery
1/4 tsp. dried parsley or 3/4 tsp. minced fresh or frozen parsley
1/8 tsp. paprika
pinch of thyme
pinch of sage

Place mushrooms, buttermilk, flour, celery, parsley, and spices in Menu-ette Skillet. Mix with small spatula. Cover skillet with lid. Cook **2 minutes (_____) at 100% power.**

8 oz. chicken with skin and bones
1/4 tsp. salt
1/8 tsp. black pepper

Remove and discard skin. Wash chicken and drain on paper towel. Sprinkle with salt and pepper. Place chicken in skillet and top with sauce. Cover skillet with lid. Cook **2:30 minutes (_____) at 100% power.** Turn chicken over with finger tongs. Replace lid. Cook **2:15 minutes (_____) at 100% power.** Let stand **5 minutes (_____).** Serve in skillet.

* To sour milk, put 1 tsp. vinegar into a measuring cup and add milk to make 1/4 cup.

CHICKEN AND BROCCOLI

3 oz. chicken with skin, fat, and bones removed

Wash chicken and pat dry with paper towel. Place in 1½-pint Menu-ette and cover with lid. Cook **1 minute (_____) at 100% power.** Place chicken on plate to cool, leaving any liquid in Menu-ette.

2 oz. fresh or frozen broccoli
1/8 tsp. salt

If using fresh broccoli, wash and chop into 1-inch pieces before placing in Menu-ette. Cover with lid. Cook **2 minutes (_____) at 100% power.** Cut chicken into 1-inch pieces (no smaller) and add to broccoli. Add salt and mix. Set aside.

3 tbsp. sour cream
1/2 tsp. minced fresh or frozen onion
3 tsp. grated Parmesan cheese
1 tsp. bread crumbs
1/8 tsp. paprika

Mix sour cream and onion in small bowl. Spread mixture over chicken with rubber spatula. Cover Menu-ette with lid. Cook **1 minute (_____) at 100% power.** Stir. Sprinkle cheese, then bread crumbs, then paprika over all. Cover Menu-ette with paper towel. Cook **1 minute (_____) at 100% power.** Let stand **1 minute (_____).** Place in small bowl and serve.

CHICKEN MARENGO

2 oz. mushrooms

Wash or brush mushrooms clean. Slice and spread on paper plate. Cover with paper towel. Cook **30 seconds (_____) at 100% power.** Set aside.

1 tsp. butter
1 tbsp. (1/3 oz.) chopped fresh or frozen onion
1/8 tsp. minced fresh or frozen garlic

Put butter, onion, and garlic into Menuette Skillet. Cook **1 minute (_____) at 100% power.** Set aside.

2-oz. tomato
1½ tbsp. dry white wine
pinch of thyme
1/2 tsp. dried parsley or 1½ tsp. minced fresh or frozen parsley

Squeeze seeds out of tomato and discard. Dice tomato and add to skillet. Add mushrooms, wine, thyme, and parsley. Cover with lid. Cook **2 minutes (_____) at 100% power.** Set aside.

8 oz. chicken with skin and bones
1/4 tsp. salt
1/8 tsp. black pepper

Wash chicken and drain on paper towel. Sprinkle with salt and pepper. Place chicken bone side up in skillet and cover with sauce. Cover skillet with lid. Cook **3 minutes (_____) at 100% power.** Turn chicken over and baste with sauce. Replace lid. Cook **2:30 minutes (_____) at 100% power.** Let stand **5 minutes (_____).** Serve in skillet.

CHICKEN PARMESAN

**8 oz. chicken with
skin and bones**
**1 tbsp. grated Parmesan
cheese**
**1 tbsp. Italian bread
crumbs**

Wash chicken and drain on paper towel. Put cheese and bread crumbs on a 12-inch piece of waxed paper. Roll chicken in mixture until coated. Place chicken skin side down in Menu-ette Skillet. Cover skillet with paper towel. Cook **2 minutes (_____) at 100% power.** Turn chicken over and sprinkle any remaining crumb mixture over chicken. Cover skillet with paper towel. Cook **2:20 minutes (_____) at 100% power.** Let stand **2 minutes (_____).** Serve in skillet.

SPICY ITALIAN CHICKEN

**8 oz. chicken with skin and
bones**

Wash chicken and place on paper towel to drain.

2 tsp. butter

Place butter in 6″ browning skillet. Cook **40 seconds (_____) at 100% power** until melted.

**2 tbsp. Italian bread
crumbs**
**1 tbsp. grated Parmesan
cheese**
pinch of salt
pinch of black pepper
**pinch of garlic powder or
1/16 tsp. minced fresh
or frozen garlic**
**1/4 tsp. dried parsley or
3/4 tsp. minced fresh
or frozen parsley**

Mix remaining ingredients on a 12-inch piece of waxed paper. Dip chicken into melted butter, then roll in bread crumb mixture. Place chicken skin side up in skillet. Cover skillet with paper towel. Cook **2 minutes (_____) at 100% power.** Turn chicken over with finger tongs. Replace paper towel. Cook **2:20 minutes (_____) at 100% power.** Let stand **2 minutes (_____).** Place on small plate and serve.

CHICKEN TERIYAKI

8 oz. chicken with skin and bones

Remove and discard skin. Wash chicken and drain on paper towel. Place in Menu-ette Skillet and set aside.

1 tbsp. teriyaki sauce
1½ tsp. water
1½ tsp. chopped green onions (with tops)

Mix remaining ingredients in custard cup. Spoon mixture over chicken. Cover skillet with lid. Cook **3 minutes** (_____) at **100% power**. Turn chicken over with finger tongs. Baste chicken with sauce. Replace lid. Cook **2:30 minutes** (_____) at **100% power**. Let stand **5 minutes** (_____). Place on small plate and serve.

MOMMA'S CHICKEN CACCIATORE

8 oz. chicken with skin and bones
1/4 tsp. salt
1/4 tsp. black pepper

Wash chicken and drain on paper towel. Sprinkle with salt and pepper and set aside.

1 tsp. vegetable oil
1 tbsp. (1/3 oz.) chopped fresh or frozen onion
4 tbsp. (4 oz.) tomato sauce
1/4 tsp. dried basil

Put oil and onion into Menu-ette Skillet. Cook **1 minute** (_____) at **100% power**. Add tomato sauce and basil. Cover skillet with lid. Cook **2 minutes** (_____) at **100% power**. Stir well. Add chicken and baste with sauce. Cover skillet with lid. Cook **2:30 minutes** (_____) at **100% power**. Let stand **4 minutes** (_____). Serve in skillet.

STUFFED CHICKEN BREAST

2 slices bacon
2 tbsp. (2/3 oz.) chopped fresh or frozen onion

Cut bacon into 1/2-inch pieces. Put pieces into 6″ browning skillet. Cover skillet with paper towel. Cook **1:45 minutes (_____) at 100% power.** Add onion to skillet. Cook **1 minute (_____) at 100% power.** Pour mixture into strainer and drain off grease. Return mixture to skillet and set aside.

1/2 cup (3/4 oz.) stuffing croutons or crumbled stale bread
1/2 cup water
1/4 tsp. thyme

Put croutons into small bowl. Add water and let stand until water is absorbed. Pour into strainer and press water out with rubber spatula. Add croutons to skillet. Add thyme and mix well with a fork. Set aside.

8 oz. chicken breast with skin and bones
1/4 tsp. salt
1/8 tsp. black pepper

Wash chicken and drain on paper towel. Lightly sprinkle bone side of breast with salt and pepper, then fill cavity with stuffing. Place chicken skin side down in skillet. Cover skillet with lid. Cook **3 minutes (_____) at 100% power.** Pour liquid out of skillet and discard.

1/8 tsp. paprika

Turn chicken over with finger tongs. Sprinkle paprika on skin side of chicken and cover skillet with paper towel. Cook **1:30 minutes (_____) at 100% power.** Let stand **1 minute (_____).** Place on small plate and serve.

BEVERAGES AND SNACKS

SPICED APPLE CIDER

1½-inch-long piece of
  cinnamon stick
5–6-oz. can (2/3 cup)
  apple juice
3 tbsp. rum

Put cinnamon stick and apple juice into
mug. Cook **1:45 minutes (_____)**
at 100% power until mixture boils.
Add rum, stir, and serve.

HOT ORANGE DRINK

1 tbsp. sugar
1/2 tsp. cornstarch
1/2 cup water

Place sugar and cornstarch in large mug.
Mix with small wire whisk. Stir in water.
Cook **1:10 minutes (_____) at**
100% power.

1 drop vanilla
1/2 cup fresh* or
  refrigerated orange juice

Add vanilla and orange juice. Cook **30**
seconds (_____) at 100% power.
Stir well with wire whisk and serve.

* A 9-oz. orange will yield 1/2 cup juice.

HOT SPICED WINE

1/2 cup dry red wine
1/4 cup water
2 tbsp. sugar
4 whole cloves
1-inch-long piece of
  cinnamon stick
1/8 tsp. lemon juice or
  1 slice lemon
1 slice orange

Combine all ingredients in Cook 'N' Pour Pan or Gravy Maker Pot. Cook **2 minutes** (_____) **at 100% power,** then cook **3 minutes** (_____) **at 30% power.** Strain mixture into mug and serve.

HOT COCOA

2 tsp. sugar
1 tsp. cocoa
1 cup milk

Combine all ingredients in mug. Cook **1:40 minutes** (_____) **at 100% power.** (Oven with probe: Cook to temperature of 140 degrees.) Stir well with spoon or small wire whisk and serve.

Variation: Hot Cocoa and Marshmallows

2 tsp. sugar
1 tsp. cocoa
1 cup milk

Combine all ingredients in mug. Cook **1:10 minutes** (_____) **at 100% power.** Stir well with spoon or small wire whisk.

15 miniature marshmallows

Place marshmallows on top of cocoa. Cook **30 seconds** (_____) **at 100% power.** Stir until marshmallows are melted.

IRISH COFFEE WITH WHIPPED CREAM

Whipped cream:
2 tbsp. heavy cream
1 tsp. powdered sugar

Chill 1-cup liquid measure and beaters from electric mixer in refrigerator for **30 minutes (_____)**. Put cream and sugar into liquid measure and beat until stiff. Place whipped cream in refrigerator until ready to add to recipe.

Coffee:
1 cup water
2 tsp. instant coffee

Pour water into 1-cup liquid measure. Cook **2:30 minutes (_____) at 100% power** until water boils. Add coffee to water and stir well. Set aside.

2 tbsp. Irish whiskey
2 tsp. brown sugar
1 maraschino cherry

Rinse an Irish coffee mug in hot water. Add whiskey and sugar to mug and stir. Add coffee and stir. Scoop whipped cream out of cup with rubber spatula. Carefully slide whipped cream off spatula onto surface of coffee. Top whipped cream with cherry. Serve with straw.

PLANTAINS

8-oz. ripe plantain
1 cup water
1 tsp. salt

Peel plantain and cut into 1/2-inch-thick slices. Place water and salt in 1½-pint mixing bowl. Add plantain slices to soak. Set aside.

1/2 cup vegetable oil
(preferably peanut oil)

Pour oil in 10" browning skillet. Cook **5 minutes (_____) at 100% power**. Place wet plantain slices in oil with finger tongs, arranging slices in a single layer. Cover skillet with paper towel. Cook **40 seconds (_____) at 100% power.** Remove paper towel and discard. Turn slices over. Cook **45 seconds (_____) at 100% power.** Drain on paper towel and serve hot.

GREEN PLANTAINS (TOSTONES)

8-oz. unripe green plantain

Cut off ends of plantain with sharp knife, then cut through skin lengthwise in 3 places. Remove and discard skin, holding plantain under running water to make peeling easier. Cut plantain into 1/2-inch-thick slices. Place on paper plate and set aside.

1/4 cup vegetable oil

Pour oil into 8½″ browning skillet. Cook **3 minutes (_____) at 100% power.** Place plantain slices in oil with finger tongs, arranging slices in a single layer. Cook **40 seconds (_____) at 100% power.** Turn slices over with finger tongs. Cook **45 seconds (_____) at 100% power.** Lay several paper towels on paper plate, then place plantain slices on towels to drain.

Cut a 6-inch piece of parchment paper. Place one slice on half of the paper and fold the other half over the slice. Press down on paper with turner to flatten slice. Return flattened slice to paper towels. Repeat for remaining slices. Heat oil again 3:30 minutes (_____) at 100% power. Place 1/3 of cooked slices in skillet with tongs. Cook **30 seconds (_____) at 100% power** until nicely browned. Turn slices over with tongs. Cook **30 seconds (_____) at 100% power.**

salt (optional)

Remove slices from skillet with tongs and place on paper plate. Immediately sprinkle with salt. Before cooking second batch, heat oil again **2 minutes (_____) at 100% power.** Repeat for third batch. Serve warm.

ROASTED CHESTNUTS

Note: Chestnuts are very low in calories because of their low fat content. Store raw chestnuts in the refrigerator for no more than a few weeks; longer storage will cause them to lose their moisture.

6 chestnuts

Carefully cut a slit in the shell of each chestnut to prevent exploding. Place chestnuts in a circle on paper plate. Cook **1:30 minutes** (_____) at **100% power.** Allow chestnuts to cool **2 minutes** (_____) before serving.

ROASTED GARBANZO BEANS

Vendors at Italian-American celebrations used to sell this snack, but now they sell popcorn instead. Today roasted garbanzo beans are considered a health food delicacy.

4 oz. dried garbanzo beans
1½ quarts water

Place beans and water in 2-quart container and soak **8 hours** (_____) or overnight.

3 cups water
1 tsp. salt (optional)

Drain beans and place in 1½-quart Corning Ware pot. Add water and salt. Cook **8 minutes** (_____) at **100% power,** then cook **20 minutes** (_____) at **50% power.** Drain beans. Spread in a single layer in a Corning Ware pie plate. Place plate in freezer and freeze until beans are white. (This may take several hours.) Remove plate from freezer and place directly in oven. Cook **5 minutes** (_____) at **100% power.** Stir. Cook **5 minutes** (_____) at **100% power.** Stir again, mixing beans well. Cook **2 minutes** (_____) at **100% power.** Store in container.

POPCORN

Note: There are special utensils and several brands of pre-packaged frozen popcorn on the market for times when you want to make a large batch of popcorn. For an occasional small serving of popcorn, prepare this recipe, which calls for a regular Corning Ware pot.

1/2 cup water

Pour water into Gravy Maker Pot. Cook **4 minutes (_____) at 100% power** to heat pot.

1 tbsp. popping corn

Discard water and place popcorn in pot. Cover with lid. Cook **5 minutes (_____) at 100% power.** All corn should pop.

2 tsp. butter*
salt to taste

Place butter in custard cup. Cook **1 minute (_____) at 100% power** until melted. Pour over popcorn. Add salt and serve.

* To eliminate the butter, spray popped popcorn with no-stick cooking spray and add salt before serving.

CAKES AND FROSTINGS

CORNBREAD

1/4 cup corn meal
2 tbsp. all-purpose flour
1 tsp. sugar*
1/8 tsp. salt
1/8 tsp. baking soda
1/4 tsp. baking powder
1 tbsp. vegetable oil
1/4 cup buttermilk or
　sour milk**

1/2 tsp. butter (optional)

Mix dry ingredients in 1-quart mixing bowl. Add oil and milk. Mix well with wire whisk.

Cut a paper towel to line a 14-oz. Pyrex Bake Mate. Pour batter into Bake Mate. Cook **1:40 minutes (_____) at 100% power,** giving Bake Mate a half-turn halfway through cooking time. (Autorotating oven: Eliminate turn.) Place Bake Mate on flat surface for **5 minutes (_____)** to finish cooking. Remove cornbread from Bake Mate. Peel off and discard paper. Place cornbread on small plate. Spread butter over cornbread and serve.

* This recipe can be made without sugar. Decrease cooking time by **10 seconds (_____).**

** To sour milk, put 1 tsp. vinegar in a measuring cup and add milk to make 1/4 cup.

SUGAR AND SPICE APPLE CAKE

1½ tbsp. butter
1/3 cup sugar
1 small egg

1/3 cup all-purpose flour
1/4 tsp. baking soda
1/2 tsp. cinnamon
pinch of salt
1/2 tsp. vanilla
3 tbsp. chopped nuts
4-oz. apple, pared and cut
   into 1/4-inch cubes

Cream butter and sugar in 1-quart mixing bowl with electric mixer. Beat in egg. Clean mixture from beaters.

Sift dry ingredients into bowl and mix with rubber spatula. Stir in vanilla, nuts, and apple. Cut a paper towel to line the bottom of a 16-oz. ceramic souffle dish. Pour batter into dish. Cut a 16-inch long piece of waxed paper and fold into fourths lengthwise to make a collar to serve as a higher rim for the dish. Fasten collar with masking tape. Cook **4 minutes (_____) at 100% power,** giving dish a quarter-turn after each minute of cooking time. (Autorotating oven: Eliminate turns.) Place dish on flat surface for **10 minutes (_____)** to finish cooking.

Remove and discard collar. Turn out cake onto plate. Remove and discard paper towel. Turn cake right side up. Serve cake plain or topped with whipped cream (see recipe) or ice cream.

APPLE STREUSEL CAKE

1/2 cup all-purpose flour
1/8 tsp. salt
2 tbsp. sugar
1/8 tsp. baking soda
1/4 tsp. baking powder
1/3 cup milk
1 tbsp. vegetable oil

Sift dry ingredients into 1-quart mixing bowl. Stir in milk and oil and mix well. Cut a paper towel to line the bottom of a 24-oz. Pyrex souffle dish. Pour batter into dish and set aside.

3 oz. apple

Peel apple, cut into quarters, and remove core. Cut quarters into 1/4-inch slices. Arrange two layers of slices on top of batter. Set aside.

1 tbsp. vegetable shortening
1 tbsp. firmly packed light brown sugar
1½ tbsp. all-purpose flour
1/2 tsp. cinnamon

Mix remaining ingredients in small bowl with small fork. Spread mixture evenly over apples. Cook **2:30 minutes** (_____) at **100% power,** giving dish a half-turn halfway through cooking time. (Autorotating oven: Eliminate turn.) Place dish on flat surface for **15 minutes** (_____) to finish cooking. Turn out cake onto plate. Remove and discard paper towel. Turn cake right side up. Cool at least **30 minutes** (_____) and serve.

BANANA CAKE

4 tsp. chopped blanched
   almonds
1/4 cup all-purpose flour
3 tbsp. graham cracker crumbs
1½ tsp. grated semi-sweet
   chocolate squares
1/2 tsp. baking powder
1/4 tsp. baking soda
1/8 tsp. salt

Mix dry ingredients in small bowl and set aside.

4 tsp. butter
2 tbsp. plus 2 tsp. sugar
1 small egg
1/4 cup mashed ripe banana
   (7-oz. banana)

Place butter in 1-quart mixing bowl. Cook **4 seconds (_____) at 100% power** to soften. Add sugar and mix until fluffy. Add egg and beat well. Add banana and beat until smooth. Mix in dry ingredients.

1/8 tsp. butter or
   shortening
1½ tsp. sugar

Grease and sugar the sides of a 24-oz. Pyrex souffle dish and cut a paper towel to line the bottom. Pour batter into dish. Cook **2:30 minutes (_____) at 100% power,** giving dish a half-turn halfway through cooking time. (Autorotating oven: Cook **2:45 minutes (_____) at 100% power,** eliminating turn.) Place dish on a flat surface for **5 minutes (_____)** to finish cooking. Turn out cake onto rack to cool. Chill thoroughly in refrigerator before serving. Serve with whipped cream topping.

Whipped cream topping:
1/4 cup heavy cream
1 tsp. powdered sugar

Place 2-cup liquid measure and the beaters from an electric mixer into refrigerator for **30 minutes (_____)** to chill. Place cream and sugar in liquid measure and beat until mixture is stiff. Spread on top of chilled pie or cake.

BLUEBERRY STREUSEL CAKE

2 oz. (1/3 cup) fresh blueberries*

Remove stems and other debris from blueberries before measuring. Wash and spread on paper towel to dry.

1 small egg, separated
1 tbsp. sugar

Set aside egg yolk in custard cup. Place egg white in 2-cup liquid measure. Beat with electric mixer until frothy. Continue to beat, adding sugar slowly, until mixture is stiff. Set aside.

2 tbsp. butter
3 tbsp. sugar
1/16 tsp. salt
1/4 tsp. vanilla

Place butter in 1-quart mixing bowl. Cook **12 seconds (_____) at 100% power** to soften. Add sugar and cream mixture with electric mixer (not necessary to clean egg white from beaters). Add salt, vanilla, and egg yolk. Beat until creamy.

3/8 cup all-purpose flour
1/8 tsp. baking powder
4 tsp. milk

Combine flour and baking powder in clean custard cup. Add to batter alternately with milk, beating well after each addition. Set aside.

1 tsp. flour

Place blueberries in emptied custard cup. Add flour and gently mix together. Add floured blueberries to batter and fold in with rubber spatula. Then fold in egg white mixture. Cut a paper towel to line bottom of a 24-oz. Pyrex souffle dish. Pour batter into dish and set aside.

1 tbsp. vegetable shortening
1 tbsp. light brown sugar
1½ tbsp. all-purpose flour
1/2 tsp. cinnamon

Mix remaining ingredients in small bowl. Sprinkle mixture evenly over top of batter. Cook **3 minutes (_____) at 100% power,** giving dish a one-third turn after each minute of cooking time. (Autorotating oven: Eliminate turns.)

(Continued on page 202)

Place dish on flat surface for **15 minutes** (_____) to finish cooking. Turn out cake onto rack to dry thoroughly before serving.

* Frozen blueberries taste the same in this recipe but make the batter harder to mix.

CARROT CAKE

4-oz. carrot

Scrub carrot with brush. Cut off and discard ends. Grate carrot and set aside.

1 small egg
1/4 cup plus 2 tbsp. sugar
1/4 cup vegetable oil

Place egg in 1-quart mixing bowl and beat slightly with electric mixer. Add sugar, oil, and carrot to bowl one at a time, mixing well after each addition.

1/4 cup plus 2 tbsp.
  all-purpose flour
2 tbsp. regular wheat germ
1/4 tsp. cinnamon
1/4 tsp. baking soda
1/8 tsp. salt
1/4 cup (1 oz.) chopped nuts

Mix dry ingredients in small bowl. Add to egg mixture and mix with electric mixer just until blended. Add nuts to batter and mix with rubber spatula. Line the bottom of a 24-oz. Pyrex souffle dish with waxed paper. Pour batter into dish. Cook **4 minutes (_____) at 100% power,** giving dish a quarter-turn after each minute of cooking time. (Autorotating oven: Cook **3:30 minutes [_____] at 100% power,** eliminating turns.) Place dish on flat surface for **10 minutes (_____)** to finish cooking.

cream cheese frosting
  (see below)

Turn out cake onto rack and cool thoroughly. Place cake on plate. Frost with cream cheese frosting.

Cream cheese frosting:
1½ oz. cream cheese
1½ oz. butter
3/4 cup powdered sugar
1/4 tsp. vanilla

Place cream cheese and butter in small bowl. Cook **2 seconds (_____) at 100% power** to soften. Beat with electric mixer. Add sugar and vanilla and beat until smooth. Spread on cooled cake.

CHEESECAKE

1½ tsp. butter
2 tbsp. graham cracker crumbs
1½ tsp. sugar
dash of cinnamon

Put butter into 16-oz. ceramic souffle dish. Cook **25 seconds (_____) at 100% power** until melted. Add graham cracker crumbs, sugar, and cinnamon to butter. Mix well with rubber spatula. Press mixture into sides and bottom of dish with greased spoon. Cook **15 seconds (_____) at 100% power.** Set aside.

1 extra-large or 2 small egg whites
1/8 tsp. vanilla
2 tbsp. sugar

Beat egg white in 2-cup liquid measure with electric mixer. Add vanilla and beat until stiff. Add sugar gradually and beat until stiff. Set aside.

4 oz. cream cheese
1 tsp. lemon juice

Put cream cheese into small bowl and beat with uncleaned beaters. Add lemon juice and beat until smooth. Add egg white and beat until smooth. Pour batter into souffle dish. Cook **4 minutes (_____) at 50% power,** giving dish a quarter-turn after each minute of cooking time. (Autorotating oven: Eliminate turns.) Place dish on flat surface for **5 minutes (_____)** to finish cooking. Loosen cake from sides of dish with small metal spatula and turn out cake onto plate. Turn cake over onto large turner or your hand and place right side up on plate. Chill thoroughly and serve.

ITALIAN CHEESECAKE

1 tbsp. minced almonds

Line bottom of 16-oz. ceramic souffle dish with almonds. Fold a 16-inch piece of waxed paper into thirds lengthwise to make a collar for outside rim of dish. Fasten collar with masking tape. Set aside.

1 small egg, separated

Place egg yolk in 1-quart mixing bowl. Set aside. Place egg white in 2-cup liquid measure. Beat until firm with electric mixer. (Do not clean beaters.) Set aside.

**6 oz. whole milk ricotta
  cheese**
pinch of salt
1 tsp. all-purpose flour
4 tsp. sugar
1 small egg yolk

Place remaining ingredients in mixing bowl with egg yolk. Beat with electric mixer at least **5 minutes (_____).** *
Fold in beaten egg white with rubber spatula. Pour batter into prepared dish, tilting dish to even out batter. Cook **3 minutes (_____) at 100% power,** giving dish a one-third turn after each minute of cooking time. (Autorotating oven: Eliminate turns.) Place dish on flat surface for **10 minutes (_____)** to finish cooking. Loosen sides and bottom of cake with small metal spatula. Turn out cake onto plate with almonds on top. Chill for **30 minutes (_____)** before serving.

* For a variation, at this point blend in 3/4 oz. milk chocolate (chopped fine) and 3/4 oz. minced maraschino cherries.

CHOCOLATE BUTTERMILK CAKE

1/3 cup all-purpose flour
1½ tbsp. cocoa
1/4 cup sugar
1/4 tsp. baking soda
1/4 tsp. salt
2½ tsp. vegetable oil
1/4 cup buttermilk or sour
   milk*

Sift dry ingredients together into 1-quart mixing bowl. Add oil and milk to bowl. Mix well with wire whisk. Line the bottom of a 14-oz. Pyrex Bake Mate with a paper towel cut to fit. Pour batter into Bake Mate. Cook **2 minutes (_____) at 100% power,** giving Bake Mate a half-turn halfway through cooking time. (Autorotating oven: Eliminate turn.) Place Bake Mate on flat surface for **5 minutes (_____)** to finish cooking.

easy milk chocolate frosting
   (see below)

Turn out cake onto rack to cool. Put cake on plate and frost with easy milk chocolate frosting.

Easy milk chocolate frosting:
1/2 cup powdered sugar
1/2 tsp. cocoa
2 tsp. vegetable oil
1/8 tsp. vanilla
2 tsp. milk

Sift together sugar and cocoa into 2-cup liquid measure. Add remaining ingredients. Mix with electric mixer on low speed until ingredients are blended. Increase speed to high and beat until frosting is smooth. (This makes a thick frosting that is best for frosting only the top of a cake.)

* To sour milk, put 1 tsp. vinegar in a measuring cup and add milk to make 1/4 cup.

CHOCOLATE SAUERKRAUT CAKE

Note: This cake is larger than the other cakes in this book, but it is an excellent way to use up leftover sauerkraut. It is especially good when chilled.

4 oz. sauerkraut

Place sauerkraut in strainer and rinse well under running water. Set aside to drain.

4 tbsp. butter
3/4 cup sugar
1 small egg
1/2 tsp. vanilla

Place butter in 1-quart mixing bowl. Cook **10 seconds (_____) at 100% power** to soften. Add sugar and beat with wire whisk until fluffy. Add egg and beat until well mixed. Stir in vanilla. Set aside.

1 cup all-purpose flour
1/4 cup cocoa
1/2 tsp. baking powder
1/2 tsp. baking soda
1/8 tsp. salt
1/3 cup water

Place dry ingredients in small bowl and mix with fork. Add dry ingredients to sugar mixture alternately with water, mixing well after each addition with rubber spatula. Set bowl aside.

Empty sauerkraut out of strainer onto paper towel. Pat with towel to remove excess moisture. Place sauerkraut on cutting board and chop very fine. Add to batter and mix well with rubber spatula.

1/8 tsp. butter or
  shortening
2 tsp. sugar

Grease and sugar the sides of a 48-oz. ceramic souffle dish. Line bottom of dish with a paper towel cut to fit. Pour batter into dish. Cook **5 minutes (_____) at 100% power,** giving dish a half-turn halfway through cooking time. (Autorotating oven: Eliminate turn.) Place dish on flat surface for **10 minutes (_____) to finish cooking.**

**chocolate sour cream
frosting (see below)**

Place plate over dish and turn cake over onto plate. Remove and discard paper towel. Place cake right side up on rack to cool. When cool, place on plate and frost with chocolate sour cream frosting. Chill cake thoroughly before serving.

Chocolate sour cream frosting:

**3 oz. semi-sweet chocolate
  squares
2 tbsp. butter
1/4 cup sour cream
1/2 tsp. vanilla
1/8 tsp. salt**

Break chocolate squares in half and place in 1-quart mixing bowl. Add butter. Cook **1 minute (_____) at 100% power.** Chocolate will be partially melted. Stir mixture with rubber spatula until chocolate is completely melted and mixture is smooth. Add sour cream, vanilla, and salt. Mix well.

1 cup powdered sugar

Place strainer over bowl and pour sugar into it. Push sugar through strainer with rubber spatula. Beat with electric mixer until very smooth. Spread over cooled cake.

 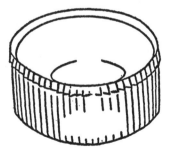

COFFEECAKE

1 tbsp. butter
1/4 cup sugar

Place butter in 1-quart mixing bowl. Cook **15 seconds** (_____) **at 100% power** to soften. Add sugar and mix with wire whisk until fluffy. Set aside.

1/3 cup all-purpose flour
1/8 tsp. baking soda
1/4 tsp. baking powder
1/8 tsp. salt

Sift dry ingredients together into small bowl. Set aside.

1/4 cup buttermilk or sour milk*
1/4 tsp. vanilla

Mix buttermilk and vanilla in 1-cup liquid measure. Add dry ingredients to sugar mixture alternately with milk, mixing well with wire whisk after each addition. Line bottom of a 14-oz. Pyrex Bake Mate with a paper towel cut to fit. Pour batter into Bake Mate. Fold a 16-inch piece of waxed paper into thirds lengthwise to form a collar for outside rim of dish. Fasten with masking tape. Set aside.

2 tsp. vegetable shortening
2 tsp. firmly packed light brown sugar
1 tbsp. all-purpose flour
1/2 tsp. cinnamon

Mix remaining ingredients in small bowl with small fork. Sprinkle mixture evenly over top of batter. Cook **2:30 minutes** (_____) **at 100% power,** giving Bake Mate a half-turn halfway through cooking time. (Autorotating oven: Eliminate turn.) Place Bake Mate on flat surface for **5 minutes** (_____) to finish cooking.

Remove and discard collar. Loosen sides of cake with small metal spatula. Turn out cake onto a piece of waxed paper. Remove and discard paper lining. Place cake right side up on rack for **15 minutes** (_____) to dry before serving.

* To sour milk, put 1 tsp. vinegar in a measuring cup and add milk to make 1/4 cup.

LEMON CAKE

2 tbsp. sugar
1/4 tsp. cinnamon
1/4 tsp. vanilla
2 tbsp. lemon juice

Mix sugar, cinnamon, vanilla, and lemon juice in custard cup. Set aside to be used later as topping.

1½ tbsp. vegetable oil
1/4 cup sugar
1 small egg
2 tbsp. milk
1/4 tsp. vanilla

Place oil, sugar, and egg in 1-quart mixing bowl. Mix with wire whisk. Set aside. Place milk and vanilla in custard cup. Set aside.

1/3 cup all-purpose flour
1/4 tsp. baking powder
1/16 tsp. salt
1/2 tsp. lemon peel

Sift dry ingredients together into small bowl. Add to egg mixture alternately with milk mixture, mixing well after each addition with wire whisk. Add lemon peel and mix well.

1/8 tsp. butter or
  shortening
1 tsp. sugar

Grease and sugar sides of a 16-oz. ceramic souffle dish. Cut a piece of waxed paper to line bottom. Pour batter into dish. Cover top of dish only with a small piece of plastic wrap. (A large piece can wrap itself under dish and keep cake from rising.) Cook **1 minute (_____) at 100% power.** Turn dish halfway around. Cook **40 seconds (_____) at 100% power.** (Autorotating oven: Eliminate turn.)

Remove plastic wrap and quickly poke holes in cake all the way to the bottom with large two-tined fork. Spoon lemon juice topping over holes, rubbing in with back of spoon until topping is completely absorbed by cake. Let stand **5 minutes (_____).** Loosen sides of cake with small metal spatula. Turn out cake onto waxed paper, then turn right side up onto small plate. Serve warm or cold.

POUND CAKE

2 tbsp. butter
2 tbsp. sugar
1 small egg

Place butter in 1-quart mixing bowl. Cook **5 seconds (_____) at 100% power** to soften. Add sugar. Beat with electric mixer until fluffy. Add egg and beat well.

1/8 tsp. vanilla
3 tbsp. all-purpose flour
pinch of salt
1/16 tsp. baking powder
1/16 tsp. mace (optional)

Add vanilla, flour, salt, baking powder, and mace. Beat until well mixed. Batter will be very thick.

1/8 tsp. butter or
** shortening**
1 tsp. sugar

Grease and sugar sides of a 16-oz. ceramic souffle dish. Cut a paper towel to line bottom of dish. Scoop up about 1/4 of batter at a time with rubber spatula and place each scoop in one section of dish until all sections are filled. Smooth out batter with spatula. Cook **2:30 minutes at 50% power,** giving dish a half-turn halfway through cooking time. (Autorotating oven: Eliminate turn.) Place dish on flat surface for **10 minutes (_____)** to finish cooking.

1/2 tsp. powdered sugar

Turn out cake onto rack to cool. Place cake on plate. Sprinkle with powdered sugar before serving.

RHUBARB PUDDING CAKE

1½ tbsp. butter
3 tbsp. sugar
1 small egg

Place butter in 1-quart mixing bowl. Cook **3 seconds (_____) at 100% power** to soften. Add sugar and beat with electric mixer until fluffy. Add egg and mix. Set aside.

1/4 cup all-purpose flour
1/4 tsp. baking powder
1/16 tsp. salt
1/4 cup milk

Sift together flour, baking powder, and salt into small mixing bowl. Add dry ingredients to butter mixture alternately with milk, mixing well after each addition. Set aside.

8 oz. rhubarb
1/4 cup firmly packed
light brown sugar
1/4 cup (1 oz.) finely
chopped pecans or
walnuts

Wash rhubarb and cut into 1/4-inch slices. Spread evenly in bottom of 24-oz. Pyrex souffle dish. Sprinkle rhubarb slices with sugar and nuts. Pour batter on top. Cook **7 minutes (_____) at 100% power,** giving dish a half-turn halfway through cooking time. (Auto-rotating oven: Eliminate turn.) Let cake cool. Serve warm or chilled.

SHOO-FLY CAKE

1/2 cup all-purpose flour
1/4 cup sugar
1/16 tsp. salt
1/8 tsp. cinnamon
1/16 tsp. ginger
dash of ground cloves
3 tbsp. chopped walnuts
2 tbsp. butter

Place flour, sugar, salt, cinnamon, ginger, cloves, and walnuts in 1-quart mixing bowl. Mix with a pastry blender. Cut in butter with pastry blender until mixture resembles coarse crumbs. Set aside 1/4 cup of mixture for topping.

1/4 cup water
2 tbsp. dark molasses
1/4 tsp. baking soda
1/8 tsp. butter or
  shortening
1½ tsp. sugar

Pour water into 1-cup liquid measure. Cook **45 seconds (_____) at 100% power** until water boils. Add molasses and baking soda. Mix together with rubber spatula. Add to dry mixture and mix. Grease and sugar sides of a 24-oz. Pyrex souffle dish. Cut a paper towel to line bottom of dish. Pour batter into dish. Sprinkle reserved crumb mixture on top. Cook **2:30 minutes (_____) at 100% power,** giving dish a half-turn halfway through cooking time. (Autorotating oven: Eliminate turn.) Place dish on flat surface for **5 minutes (_____)** to finish cooking.

1 tsp. powdered sugar

Turn out cake onto rack to cool. Place cake on plate. Sift powdered sugar over top before serving.

SPICE LEFTOVER CAKE

1 tbsp. vegetable shortening
1/4 cup water
2 tbsp. raisins

Place shortening, water, and raisins in 1-quart mixing bowl. Cook **1 minute (_____) at 100% power.** Set aside to cool.

1 cup all-purpose flour 1/2 tsp. baking powder 1/4 tsp. nutmeg 1/4 tsp. cinnamon 1/4 tsp. cloves dash of salt	Sift together flour, baking powder, and spices into small bowl and set aside.
1/2 cup firmly packed dark brown sugar 1½ tbsp. dark molasses 1 cup cake crumbs* 1/8 tsp. butter or shortening 1½ tsp. sugar	Add brown sugar and molasses to shortening mixture. Mix well with wire whisk. Add dry ingredients and mix well with rubber spatula. Add cake crumbs and mix well. Grease and sugar a 24-oz. Pyrex souffle dish. Cut a paper towel to line bottom of dish. Pour batter into dish. Cook **3:10 minutes (_____) at 100% power,** giving dish a half-turn halfway through cooking time. (Autorotating oven: Eliminate turn.) Place dish on flat surface for **5 minutes (_____)** to finish cooking.
glossy chocolate icing (see below)	Turn out cake onto rack to cool. Place cake on plate and frost with glossy chocolate icing before serving.
Glossy chocolate icing: 1½ tsp. butter 1/2 oz. unsweetened chocolate	Place butter and chocolate in 1½-pint Menu-ette. Cook **1 minute (_____) at 100% power.** Chocolate will be partially melted. Spear unmelted chocolate with fork and swirl it around Menu-ette until it melts completely.
1½ tsp. warm water 1/2 tsp. vanilla 1/2 cup powdered sugar	Add water and vanilla. Stir with wire whisk. Sift sugar into mixture and stir until smooth enough to spread. If mixture is too thick, add a little more water.

* Any cake crumbs will do. This is a good way to use up any cake hardened from overcooking in the microwave oven.

WALNUT TORTE

1 small egg
1/4 cup sugar
1/4 cup graham cracker
   crumbs
2 tbsp. finely chopped
   walnuts or pecans
vanilla ice cream or whipped
   cream (optional)

Place all ingredients in 2-cup liquid measure. Beat with electric mixer until well mixed. Pour into 1-pint Menu-ette. Cook **1:50 minutes (_____) at 100% power,** giving Menu-ette a half-turn halfway through cooking time. (Auto-rotating oven: Eliminate turn.) Let stand **10 minutes (_____)** to cool. Turn out onto plate. Serve topped with vanilla ice cream or whipped cream (see recipe).

WHITE CAKE

1 tbsp. butter
1/4 cup sugar

Place butter in 1-quart mixing bowl. Cook **15 seconds (_____) at 100% power** to soften. Add sugar and mix well with wire whisk until fluffy. Set aside.

1/3 cup all-purpose flour
1/8 tsp. baking soda
1/4 tsp. baking powder
1/8 tsp. salt
1/4 cup buttermilk or
** sour milk***
1/4 tsp. vanilla

Sift together dry ingredients into small bowl and set aside. Place buttermilk and vanilla in 1-cup liquid measure and stir. Add dry ingredients to butter mixture alternately with milk, mixing well with wire whisk after each addition. Cut a paper towel to line bottom of a 14-oz. Pyrex Bake Mate. Pour batter into Bake Mate. Cook **2:30 minutes (_____) at 100% power,** giving Bake Mate a half-turn halfway through cooking time. (Autorotating oven: Eliminate turn.) Place Bake Mate on flat surface for **5 minutes (_____)** to finish cooking.

milk chocolate frosting
** (see below)**

Turn out cake onto rack to cool. Place cake on plate and frost with milk chocolate frosting.

Milk chocolate frosting:
4 tsp. milk

Pour milk into custard cup. Cook **17 seconds (_____) at 100% power** to scald. Set aside.

2½ tsp. vegetable
** shortening**
1 tbsp. cocoa
1/2 cup powdered sugar
1/4 tsp. vanilla

Mix shortening and cocoa in 1½-pint bowl. Add sugar, vanilla, and milk. Set bowl inside 1½-quart bowl half-filled with ice water. Beat mixture with electric mixer until frosting is smooth, thick, and light brown.

2 tbsp. powdered sugar

Add sugar to thicken frosting as desired. Frost cooled cake.

* To sour milk, put 1 tsp. vinegar in a measuring cup and add milk to make 1/4 cup.

COOKIES AND CANDY

CHOCOLATE COOKIES

1/2 oz. unsweetened chocolate

Place chocolate on open wrapper or in custard cup. Cook **2 minutes (_____) at 100% power** until melted.

1 cup all-purpose flour
1/8 tsp. baking soda
1/4 tsp. salt

Mix flour, baking soda, and salt in 1½-pint mixing bowl. Set aside.

1/2 cup (1 stick) butter
1/3 cup firmly packed dark brown sugar
1 small egg
1/2 tsp. vanilla

Place butter in 1-quart mixing bowl. Cook **10 seconds (_____) at 100% power** to soften. Add brown sugar and beat well with electric mixer. Add egg, vanilla, and melted chocolate. Mix well. Add dry ingredients and blend with mixer.

1/4 cup sugar

Place sugar in small, shallow dessert bowl. Place paper towel on 11″ ceramic plate. Scoop up 1 tbsp. batter and drop into sugar. Roll cookie in sugar with fingers until completely coated. Place on plate. Repeat until a batch of 8 cookies is prepared. Arrange in circle on plate. Cook **2 minutes (_____) at 100% power,** giving plate a half-turn halfway through cooking time. Let stand **1 minute (_____)** to allow cookies to harden.

(Continued on page 218)

Slide paper towel off plate. Peel cookies away from paper towel and place on rack to dry moist bottoms. Discard paper towel. Place another paper towel on plate and cook next batch of cookies. Repeat for third batch. (Recipe makes 24 cookies in all.) Store cookies in airtight container.

CHOCOLATE CHIP COOKIES

1/2 cup (1 stick) butter

Place butter in 1-quart mixing bowl. Cook **10 seconds (_____) at 100% power** to soften.

1/4 cup sugar
1/2 tsp. vanilla
1 cup plus 3 tbsp.
  all-purpose flour
1/3 cup chopped nuts
4 oz. (2/3 cup) milk
  chocolate chips

Add sugar and vanilla. Beat with electric mixer until creamy. Add flour and nuts. Mix well with mixer until mixture resembles coarse crumbs. Add chocolate chips and blend in with hands. Place paper towel on 11" ceramic plate. Scoop up a level tbsp. of batter. With small spatula pry batter loose and place on plate. Repeat until a batch of 8 cookies is prepared. Arrange in circle on plate. Cook **2 minutes (_____)* at 100% power,** giving plate a half-turn halfway through cooking time.

Slide paper towel off plate. Let stand **2 minutes (_____)** to allow cookies to harden. Peel away from paper towel and place on rack to dry. Discard paper towel. Place another paper towel on plate and cook next batch of 8 cookies. Repeat for third batch. (Recipe makes 24 cookies in all.) When cookies are thoroughly cooled, store in airtight container.

* If centers of any of the cookies are brown, reduce cooking time.

GINGERSNAPS

3/8 cup vegetable shortening
2 tbsp. molasses
1/2 cup firmly packed dark
   brown sugar
1 small egg

Place shortening, molasses, sugar, and egg in 1-quart mixing bowl. Beat well with electric mixer. Set aside.

1½ cups all-purpose flour
1 tsp. baking soda
1/4 tsp. salt
1/2 tsp. cinnamon
1/2 tsp. ginger
1/2 tsp. ground cloves

Sift together dry ingredients into 1½-pint mixing bowl. Add to sugar mixture. Mix on low speed until thoroughly blended. Place piece of waxed paper on 11" ceramic plate. Scoop up 2 tsp. batter and place in palm of one hand. Flatten into disk shape by pressing both palms together. Repeat until 8 cookies are prepared. Arrange cookies in a circle on plate. Cook **2 minutes (_____) at 100% power,** giving plate a half-turn halfway through cooking time. (Autorotating oven: Eliminate turn.)

Slide paper off plate. Peel cookies off paper and place on rack to cool. Discard paper. Place another piece of waxed paper on plate and cook next batch. Repeat for third batch. (Recipe makes 24 cookies in all.) When cookies are thoroughly cooled, store in airtight container.

LADYFINGERS

2 tsp. butter

Place butter in custard cup. Cook **20 seconds** (_____) **at 100% power** until melted. Set aside.

1 small egg white
2 tbsp. sugar
1/8 tsp. vanilla
1/8 tsp. orange peel
4 tsp. all-purpose flour

Place egg white in 2-cup liquid measure. Beat with electric mixer until stiff. Gradually add sugar and beat until stiff. Add vanilla and orange peel. Fold in with rubber spatula. Add flour and fold in with spatula. Fold in melted butter. Place sheet of waxed paper on 11″ ceramic platter. Scoop up a level tbsp. of batter and scrape onto waxed paper with small spatula. Repeat for 3 other cookies. Cook **1:20 minutes** (_____) **at 100% power,** giving platter a half-turn halfway through cooking time.

Slide paper off plate and let stand exactly **1 minute** (_____). Pull paper away from each cookie and place cookies on rack to cool. Discard paper and place another on plate to cook remaining 4 cookies. (Recipe makes 8 cookies in all.) Store in airtight container.

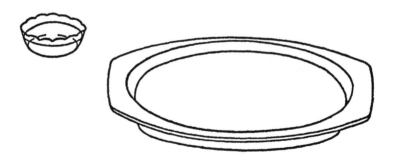

LEMON WAFERS

6 tbsp. butter
6 tbsp. sugar
1 small egg
1/4 tsp. vanilla
1/4 tsp. lemon juice
2 tbsp. milk

Place butter in 1-quart mixing bowl. Cook **7 seconds (_____) at 100% power** to soften. Add sugar and beat well with electric mixer. Add egg, vanilla, lemon juice, and milk. Beat until well mixed. Set aside.

1 cup all-purpose flour
1/2 tsp. baking powder
1/8 tsp. baking soda
1/4 tsp. salt

Sift together dry ingredients into 1½-pint mixing bowl. Add half of dry ingredients at a time to butter mixture, blending well with electric mixer on low speed after each addition.

1/4 cup sugar
1/2 tsp. grated or dry
  lemon peel

Mix sugar and lemon peel in small, shallow bowl. Place paper towel on 11″ ceramic plate. Scoop up 1 tbsp. batter and drop into sugar mixture. Coat well with sugar and place on paper towel. Repeat for 5 more cookies, arranging the 6 cookies in a circle on plate. Cook **1:30 minutes (_____) at 100% power,** giving plate a half-turn halfway through cooking time. (Autorotating oven: Eliminate turn.) Let stand **1 minute (_____).**

Gently slide paper towel off plate. Peel cookies off paper towel and place on rack to harden. Discard paper towel. Place another paper towel on plate and cook next batch of cookies. Repeat for 2 remaining batches. (Recipe makes 24 cookies in all.) It is not necessary to store these cookies in an airtight container.

BROWNIES

2 tbsp. butter

Place butter in custard cup. Cook **15 seconds** (_____) **at 100% power** until partially melted. Set aside.

1 small egg
1/4 cup sugar
1/8 tsp. salt
1/4 tsp. vanilla
3 tbsp. all-purpose flour
2 tbsp. cocoa
2 tbsp. (1/2 oz.) chopped nuts
2 tbsp. (1 oz.) semi-sweet chocolate chips

Place egg, sugar, salt, and vanilla in 1-quart mixing bowl. Beat with electric mixer at medium speed for **1 minute** (_____). Add melted butter and beat until well blended. Add flour and cocoa. Blend at low speed. Stir in nuts and chocolate chips.

1/8 tsp. butter

Butter sides of Corning Ware Petite Pan. Cut a paper towel to line bottom. Scoop up about 1/4 of batter at a time with rubber spatula and place each scoop in one corner of dish. Smooth out batter with spatula. Cook **1:45 minutes** (_____) **at 100% power,** giving pan 3 quarter-turns during cooking time. Place pan on flat surface for exactly **15 minutes** (_____) to finish cooking. Turn out brownies onto plate and remove paper towel. Turn right side up. Cut into 6 brownies and serve.

MARSHMALLOW-PECAN CANDY

Note: This recipe can be halved. Reduce cooking time for chocolate mixture to **55 seconds (_____) at 100% power.**

1/4 cup (1½ oz.) semi-sweet chocolate chips
1/4 cup (1½ oz.) butterscotch morsels
1 cup (2 oz.) miniature marshmallows

Place chips and morsels in 1½-pint mixing bowl. Cook **1:10 minutes (_____) at 100% power.** Stir until smooth. Add marshmallows. Stir until well mixed.

18 pecan halves (1 oz.)

Cover a large platter with waxed paper. Spoon about 6 marshmallows onto waxed paper and place one pecan half on top. Repeat until there are 18 candies. Place platter in refrigerator for **15 minutes (_____)** to harden. Store in refrigerator.

PEANUT BRITTLE

2 tbsp. light corn syrup
1/4 cup sugar
2 pinches salt
1/3 cup (2 oz.) salted or unsalted roasted peanuts

Place corn syrup in 2-cup liquid measure, scraping measuring spoon clean each time. Add sugar and salt. Mix well. Cook **1:15 minutes (_____) at 100% power.** Add peanuts and mix thoroughly. Cook **1:15 minutes (_____) at 100% power.**

1 tsp. butter
1/4 tsp. vanilla
1/4 tsp. baking soda

Add remaining ingredients. Stir quickly and thoroughly. Before brittle hardens, spread on buttered metal cookie sheet or unbuttered non-stick cookie sheet.* Let stand **5 minutes (_____).** Break into pieces and store in airtight jar.

* Do not use glass baking dish. Even tempered glass like Pyrex may break as candy hardens.

PIES

Today several different types of individually packaged pie pieces are available in stores. The frozen type just needs to be unsealed and heated for **30 seconds** (_____). Apple, pecan, chocolate, and cherry are some of the varieties available in this form. However, my personal favorites are not available as frozen pieces, so I've devised the following recipes.

The pie crust recipe makes enough dough for one small pie or one batch of tartlets. The pie recipes are intended as starting points from which you can go on to create pies with your favorite fillings.

PIE CRUST

1/4 cup all-purpose flour
1/16 tsp. salt
2 tbsp. vegetable shortening

Place flour and salt in 1½-pint mixing bowl. Cut in shortening with pastry blender.

2 tsp. cold water
2 drops yellow food coloring
2 drops red food coloring
1 drop green food coloring

Place water in custard cup and add food coloring. Mix until water is an even brown color. Sprinkle water over flour mixture. Mix lightly with small fork. Knead dough with hands until color is evenly distributed. Place dough in plastic bag and chill **30 minutes** (_____).

1 tsp. all-purpose flour
    (for rolling out dough)

Spread some of 1 tsp. flour on 12-inch piece of waxed paper. Dust hands with additional flour. Place dough on waxed paper and flatten with palm of hand. Sprinkle some of 1 tsp. flour on top of dough. Roll dough with rolling pin into a circle 1½-inches larger than rim of 6" Pyrex pie plate. Roll carefully from center of dough out toward edges, but

(Continued on page 226)

stop short of edges to keep from rolling them too thin. Sprinkle rest of 1 tsp. flour over dough and turn dough over several times during rolling process.
Roll dough onto rolling pin and unroll on top of pie plate. Fit crust into plate. Do not stretch dough. Push dough down into plate or crust will shrink and lose its pie shape as it cooks. Form standard fluted edge by taking the excess dough hanging over the edge of the pie plate and tucking it under itself to make a double thickness, then pinching into points with fingers. Prick crust with fork in several places, especially where side and bottom meet. (Ceramic pie weights may be used to keep sides of crust from slipping down or bubbling out.) Cook **1:45 minutes** (_____) **at 100% power.** Underside of crust will look dry when properly cooked.

COTTAGE CHEESE PIE

pie crust (see recipe)

Cook pie crust according to recipe. Set aside.

1 **extra-large egg**
3/4 **cup (7 oz.) cottage cheese**
3 **tbsp. sugar**
2 **tsp. all-purpose flour**
1 **tsp. lemon juice**
1/8 **tsp. lemon peel**

Place ingredients in blender and blend just until mixed, or mix with electric mixer for **5 minutes** (_____). Pour mixture into pie crust. Cook **6:30 minutes** (_____) **at 100% power** until knife inserted near center comes out clean. Chill thoroughly before serving.

PEANUT BUTTER PIE

pie crust (see recipe)

Cook pie crust according to recipe. Set aside.

2 tbsp. powdered sugar
1 tbsp. peanut butter

Place sugar and peanut butter in small, shallow bowl. Mix with small fork or two-tined fork. Set aside 1 tbsp. of mixture and spread remaining mixture over bottom of pie crust. Set aside.

2/3 cup milk

Pour milk into 1-cup liquid measure. Cook **1:20 minutes (_____) at 100% power** to warm. Set aside.

1/4 cup sugar
4 tsp. cornstarch
1/8 tsp. salt

Place sugar, cornstarch, and salt in 1-quart mixing bowl. Mix with wire whisk. Set aside.

1 extra-large egg yolk or
  2 small egg yolks
1/4 tsp. vanilla
2 tsp. butter

Place egg yolk in small mixing bowl. Add milk gradually, stirring constantly with wire whisk. Add mixture to dry ingredients and stir well with whisk. Cook **1:30 minutes (_____) at 100% power.** Add vanilla and butter to batter and beat with wire whisk until butter melts.

Spread batter on top of sugar mixture in pie crust. Sprinkle reserved sugar mixture on top. Cook **1 minute (_____) at 100% power.** Chill thoroughly in refrigerator.

whipped cream (optional)

Serve as is or topped with whipped cream (see recipe).

SWEET POTATO PIE

7-oz. sweet potato

Wash potato and pierce through with large two-tined fork. Place on oven tray or oven bottom. Cook **2 minutes (_____) at 100% power.** Turn potato over. Cook **1:15 minutes (_____) at 100% power** or until potato tests soft when pierced with toothpick. Wrap potato in aluminum foil and set aside.

pie crust (see recipe)

Cook pie crust according to recipe. Set aside.

2 tsp. butter
1/4 cup sugar
1 small egg
1/4 tsp. cinnamon
1/4 tsp. nutmeg
1/8 tsp. ginger
1/16 tsp. salt
1/3 cup milk

Unwrap potato and cut in half. Scoop out insides with small spoon. Measure 1/2 cup of potato and place in 1-quart mixing bowl. Beat with electric mixer until smooth. Add butter and sugar. Blend well. Add egg and beat with mixer until smooth. Blend in spices and milk.

whipped cream (optional)

Pour mixture into pie crust. Filling will come to edge of crust but will not boil over during cooking. Cook **4:30 minutes (_____) at 100% power,** giving plate a half-turn halfway through cooking time. Pie is done when knife inserted near center comes out clean. Chill thoroughly. Serve as is or with whipped cream (see recipe).

PECAN TARTLETS

pie crust dough (see recipe)

Wrap dough in plastic wrap and place in refrigerator to chill.

16 3-oz. paper cups

Using small scissors, cut away top half of each cup, leaving bottoms and 1/2 inch of sides intact. Set aside.
Fold paper towel in half four times. Press down on towel with 2″ biscuit cutter to imprint a circle. Cut circle through all thicknesses to make 16 paper circles. Set aside.

Remove dough from refrigerator and roll out into a 9-inch circle. Cut out 16 circles of dough with 2″ biscuit cutter. Place a dough circle on each paper circle and together gently shape to line a paper cup. Repeat for remaining dough, paper circles, and cups. Arrange 16 cups in a large circle on oven tray or bottom of oven. Cook **1:45 minutes (_____) at 100% power.** Allow to cool **5 minutes (_____).** Carefully remove crusts from cups and discard paper liners. Place on plate. Deflate any bubbles in crusts with small pointed knife, leaving any crumbs in crusts. Set aside.

2 tsp. butter
1/2 tsp. all-purpose flour
1 small egg
1/4 cup dark corn syrup
2 tsp. brown sugar
1 tsp. praline liqueur or cognac
1/4 cup (1 oz.) chopped pecans

Place remaining ingredients into 2-cup liquid measure and mix well. Cook **30 seconds (_____) at 100% power.** Stir until butter is blended in. Cook **40 seconds (_____) at 100% power** until mixture boils. Stir well. Fill each tartlet carefully with a tsp. of mixture. Place on plate and chill in refrigerator.

whipped cream (optional)

Serve as is or top with whipped cream (see recipe).

PUDDINGS AND CUSTARDS

OLD-FASHIONED BREAD PUDDING

1 cup water
1/2 tsp. salt
1½ oz. stale white bread,
  cut into chunks*

Combine water and salt in 1-quart mixing bowl. Soak bread in water. Pour contents of bowl into strainer and squeeze water out of bread. Set aside.

1/3 cup milk

Pour milk into 1-cup liquid measure. Cook **45 seconds (_____) at 100% power.** Set aside.

1 small egg
1 tbsp. sugar
1/8 tsp. cinnamon
1/8 tsp. lemon juice

Place egg in emptied mixing bowl and beat with wire whisk. Add sugar, cinnamon, lemon juice, and warm milk. Stir well with whisk. Add bread and mix well. Pour mixture into 8-oz. ceramic custard cup. Set aside.

1 cup water

Pour water into 1-pint Menu-ette. Cook **2:30 minutes (_____) at 100% power** until water boils. Carefully place custard cup in hot water. Cook **1:30 minutes (_____) at 100% power.** Turn Menu-ette halfway around. Cook **1 minute (_____) at 100% power.** (Autorotating oven: Eliminate turn.) Carefully remove custard cup from water and place on rack for **20 minutes (_____)** to cool. Serve warm or thoroughly chilled.

* If bread is not stale, cook **1 minute (_____) at 100% power.** Set aside on rack to cool and dry before starting the recipe.

CHOCOLATE BREAD PUDDING

1 cup water
1 tsp. salt
1¼ oz. stale white bread,
  cut into chunks*

Combine water and salt in small mixing bowl. Soak bread in water. Pour contents of bowl into strainer and squeeze water out of bread. Set aside.

1/3 cup milk
1 tbsp. chocolate syrup

Place milk and syrup in 1-cup liquid measure and stir. Cook **45 seconds** (_____) **at 100% power.** Set aside.

1 small egg
1 tbsp. sugar
1/4 tsp. cinnamon
1/2 tsp. vanilla

Place egg in 1-quart mixing bowl. Beat with wire whisk. Add sugar, cinnamon, vanilla, and warm milk. Stir well with whisk. Add bread and mix well. Pour mixture into 8-oz. ceramic custard cup. Set aside.

1 cup water

Pour water into 1-pint Menu-ette. Cook **2:30 minutes** (_____) **at 100% power** until water boils. Carefully place custard cup in hot water. Cook **2:20 minutes** (_____) **at 100% power,** giving Menu-ette a half-turn halfway through cooking time. (Autorotating oven: Cook **2:40 minutes** (_____) **at 100% power,** eliminating turn.) Carefully remove custard cup from water and place on rack **30 minutes** (_____) to cool. Serve warm or thoroughly chilled.

* If bread is not stale, cook **40 seconds** (_____) **at 100% power.** Set aside on rack to cool and dry before starting the recipe.

MOMMA'S PUDDING

1/2 cup milk
2-inch-long piece of
cinnamon stick

Place milk in 2-cup liquid measure. Add cinnamon stick. Cook **1 minute (_____) at 100% power.** Set aside.

1 tbsp. all-purpose flour
1 tbsp. sugar

Mix flour and sugar in 1-quart mixing bowl with wire whisk. Gradually add to milk and blend well with whisk. Set aside.

1 small egg yolk

Place egg yolk in emptied bowl and beat with whisk. Add milk mixture very slowly, stirring continuously. Mix well. Cook **30 seconds (_____) at 100% power.** Stir again. Cook **40 seconds (_____) at 100% power.** Remove and discard cinnamon stick. Stir well with whisk, then pour into 6- or 8-oz. custard cup. Chill before serving.

CARAMEL PUDDING

2 tbsp. heavy cream
1/4 cup milk

Pour cream and milk into 1-cup liquid measure. Set aside.

1/4 cup sugar

Place sugar in 6" browning skillet. Cook **4 minutes (_____) at 100% power,** watching carefully for first bubble of brown; stop cooking immediately when it appears. Shake skillet back and forth until sugar is a uniform golden brown. Add cream mixture gradually, stirring constantly with wire whisk. Cook **1 minute (_____) at 100% power,** stirring once during cooking time. Set aside.

2 tbsp. milk
1 tbsp. cornstarch
pinch of salt

Place milk, cornstarch, and salt in custard cup. Stir well. Stir mixture in skillet with whisk and gradually add milk mixture to skillet, stirring continuously. Cook **45 seconds (_____) at 100% power,** stirring once during cooking time.

1/4 tsp. vanilla
1 drop almond extract

Stir in vanilla and almond extracts and mix well with whisk. Pour into 6- or 8-oz. custard cup. Serve at room temperature or chilled.

CHOCOLATE PUDDING

1/2 cup milk

Pour milk into 1-quart mixing bowl. Cook **45 seconds (_____) at 100% power.** Set aside.

1½ tbsp. all-purpose flour
2 tbsp. sugar
1 tbsp. cocoa
pinch of salt

Mix dry ingredients in 1-cup liquid measure with small wire whisk. Add to warm milk and stir with whisk. Set aside.

1 egg yolk (extra-large or small)

Beat egg yolk in emptied liquid measure with whisk. Slowly add about 1/2 cup of milk mixture to egg yolk, stirring constantly with whisk. Add to milk in mixing bowl and stir with large wire whisk. Cook **40 seconds (_____) at 100% power.** Beat well with whisk. Cook **30 seconds (_____) at 100% power.** Beat again with whisk. Pour into 6- or 8-oz. custard cup. Serve warm or chilled.

FLUFFY CHOCOLATE PUDDING

1/2 cup milk

Pour milk into 1-quart mixing bowl. Cook **45 seconds (_____) at 100% power.** Set aside.

1½ tbsp. all-purpose flour
2 tbsp. sugar
1 tbsp. cocoa
pinch of salt

Mix dry ingredients in 1½-pint mixing bowl with wire whisk. Add to warm milk and stir with whisk. Set aside.

1 small egg, separated

Put egg white into 2-cup liquid measure and set aside. Put egg yolk into emptied mixing bowl and stir with whisk. Slowly add 1/2 cup of milk mixture to egg yolk, stirring continuously with whisk. Add to milk in bowl and stir well. Cook **40 seconds (_____) at 100% power.** Beat with whisk. Cook **30 seconds (_____) at 100% power.** Beat again until well mixed. Set aside.

Beat egg white with electric mixer just until stiff. Add to cooked pudding, beating with whisk until no white shows in pudding. Pour into 8-oz. custard cup. Serve warm or chilled.

LEMON PUDDING

1 small egg
2 tbsp. plus 2 tsp. sugar
1 tbsp. all-purpose flour*
1 tbsp. lemon juice
1/8 tsp. grated lemon rind
  or dried lemon peel
3 tbsp. milk

Place egg, sugar, and flour in 2-cup liquid measure. Beat with electric mixer until thick. Add lemon juice and lemon rind and mix. Add milk and beat until well mixed. Pour into 8-oz. ceramic custard cup. Set aside.

1 cup water

Pour water into 1½-pint Menu-ette. Cook **1 minute (_____) at 100% power.** Carefully place custard cup in hot water. Cook **55 seconds (_____) at 100% power.** Turn Menu-ette halfway around. Cook **50 seconds (_____) at 100% power.** Serve warm or chilled. If chilled pudding is weepy when eaten, increase cooking time a little next time so pudding will stay firm when chilled.

* For a more cakelike pudding, increase flour to 3 tbsp. Cooking time remains the same.

MOMMA'S RICE PUDDING

1/3 cup water
1/16 tsp. salt
1/8 tsp. vegetable oil
1 tbsp. long grain or
    converted white rice

Pour water into 1-pint Menu-ette. Cook **1 minute (_____) at 100% pow-er.** Add salt, oil, and rice and stir. Cook **10 minutes (_____) at 50% pow-er.** Cover with lid and set aside.

1/3 cup milk

Pour milk into 1-cup liquid measure. Cook **45 seconds (_____) at 100% power.** Set aside.

1 small egg
2 tsp. sugar
1/8 tsp. vanilla
dash of salt

Beat egg in 1½-pint mixing bowl with wire whisk. Add sugar, vanilla, and salt. Mix with whisk. Slowly add milk and stir. Drain rice into strainer, then place in 6- or 8-oz. custard cup. Add milk mixture to cup and mix with small fork.

cinnamon

Dust top of pudding with cinnamon by inserting dull knife into spice container, then gently tapping knife across top of cup. Repeat until a fine coating of cin-namon covers top of pudding. Set aside.

1 cup water

Rinse out emptied Menu-ette and pour in water. Cook **2:30 minutes (_____) at 100% power.** Carefully place cus-tard cup in hot water. Cook **1:30 min-utes (_____) at 100% power.** To keep rice from settling to bottom of cup, stir only bottom of pudding with small fork by holding fork handle against the cup rim and rotating tines only. Cook **1:30 minutes (_____) at 100% power.** Carefully remove custard cup from water and place on rack to cool. Let stand **30 minutes (_____).** Serve warm or chilled.

FLUFFY VANILLA PUDDING

1/2 cup milk

Pour milk into 1-quart mixing bowl. Cook **45 seconds (_____) at 100% power.**

1½ tbsp. all-purpose flour
1½ tbsp. sugar

Place flour and sugar in 1-cup liquid measure. Mix with small wire whisk. Add to warm milk and stir with large wire whisk.

1 small egg, separated
1/8 tsp. vanilla

Place egg white in 2-cup liquid measure and set aside. Place egg yolk in emptied 1-cup liquid measure and beat with small whisk. Gradually add some of milk mixture to egg yolk and mix well. Add egg yolk to milk mixture in large bowl and stir with large whisk. Add vanilla and mix well. Cook **40 seconds (_____) at 100% power.** Beat with large whisk. Cook **30 seconds (_____) at 100% power.** Beat again with whisk and set aside.

Beat egg white with electric mixer just until stiff. Add to milk mixture and beat with large whisk until thoroughly mixed. Pour into 8-oz. custard cup. Chill before serving.

CUSTARD

1/3 cup milk

Pour milk into 1-cup liquid measure. Cook **45 seconds (_____) at 100% power.** Set aside.

1 small egg
2 tsp. sugar
pinch of salt
1/8 tsp. vanilla
cinnamon

Place egg in 1½-pint mixing bowl. Beat with wire whisk. Add sugar, salt, and vanilla. Beat well. Gradually add warm milk and beat with whisk. Pour mixture into 8-oz. ceramic custard cup. Dust top of pudding with cinnamon by inserting dull knife into spice container, then gently tapping knife across top of cup. Repeat until a fine coating of cinnamon covers top of pudding. Set aside.

1 cup water

Pour water into 1-pint Menu-ette. Cook **2:30 minutes (_____) at 100% power** until water boils. Carefully place custard cup in water. Cook **1:30 minutes (_____) at 100% power,** giving Menu-ette a half-turn halfway through cooking time. (Autorotating oven: Eliminate turn.) Remove custard cup from water and place on rack for **20 minutes (_____)** to cool. Serve warm or chilled.

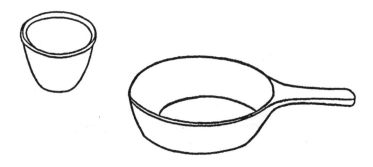

CHOCOLATE CUSTARD

1/3 cup milk

Pour milk into 1-cup liquid measure. Cook **45 seconds (_____) at 100% power.** Set aside.

1 small egg
2 tsp. sugar
1 tbsp. chocolate syrup
pinch of salt
1/8 tsp. vanilla

Place egg, sugar, chocolate syrup, salt, and vanilla in 1½-pint mixing bowl. Beat with wire whisk. Gradually add warm milk and beat until well mixed. Pour mixture into 8-oz. ceramic custard cup. Set aside.

1 cup water

Pour water into 1-pint Menu-ette. Cook **2:30 minutes (_____) at 100% power** until water boils. Carefully place custard cup in water. Cook **1:10 minutes (_____) at 100% power.** Turn Menu-ette halfway around. Cook **1 minute (_____) at 100% power.** (Auto-rotating oven: Cook **1:50 minutes (_____) at 100% power,** eliminating turn.) Carefully remove custard cup from water and place on rack for **20 minutes (_____)** to cool. Serve warm or chilled.

CHOCOLATE MOUSSE

1 extra-large egg, separated

Place egg yolk in custard cup and egg white in 2-cup liquid measure. Set aside.

1 oz. semi-sweet baking chocolate
1 tbsp. butter

Place chocolate and butter in 1-quart mixing bowl. Cook **1:10 minutes (_____) at 100% power.** Stir chocolate with wooden spoon until completely melted and mixed with butter. Add egg yolk and mix thoroughly. Leave spoon in bowl and place bowl in refrigerator for **15 minutes (_____) to cool.**

1/2 tbsp. cognac or brandy

Remove bowl from refrigerator. Add cognac and stir. Beat egg white with electric mixer until stiff. Fold egg white into chocolate mixture with rubber spatula until all traces of white disappear. Mousse will be color of milk chocolate. Scrape into 8-oz. dessert dish and place in refrigerator for at least **1 hour (_____).** The longer the mousse sits, the darker it will become; for the best possible taste, refrigerate for 24 hours before serving.

vanilla ice cream or whipped cream (optional)

Serve plain as a topping for vanilla ice cream, or topped with whipped cream (see recipe).

APPLE-CHERRY GELATIN

1 tsp. unflavored gelatin
2 tsp. sugar
4.2-oz. bottle apple-cherry
  juice (for babies)
4 drops red food coloring
  (optional)
whipped cream (optional)

Place gelatin, sugar, and half the juice in 1-cup liquid measure. Mix well with rubber spatula. Cook **40 seconds** (_____) **at 100% power** until mixture boils. Stir well with spatula so that no gelatin remains unmixed on sides and bottom. Add remaining juice and food coloring and mix well. Pour into 6- or 8-oz. custard cup. Refrigerate **1½ hours** (_____) until gelatin is firm. Serve as is or topped with whipped cream (see recipe).

Variation: Any favorite juice such as cranapple, cranberry, or grape can be substituted for the apple-cherry juice. Use 1/2 cup plus 1 tbsp. juice.

TAPIOCA FLUFF

Note: When recipe is doubled, tapioca is less fluffy but still excellent. Use 2-quart mixing bowl and increase cooking time to **6:10 minutes** (_____) **at 100% power.**

1 small egg, separated
1 tbsp. sugar
1/16 tsp. salt
1 cup milk
1½ tbsp. quick-cooking tapioca

Place egg white in 2-cup liquid measure and set aside. Place egg yolk in 1-quart mixing bowl. Add sugar, salt, milk, and tapioca to egg yolk and stir with wire whisk. Set aside for **3 minutes** (_____). Cook **4 minutes** (_____) **at 100% power.**

1 tbsp. sugar
1/4 tsp. vanilla
1 maraschino cherry

While mixture cooks, add sugar to egg white. Beat with electric mixer until stiff. Stir egg yolk mixture with whisk. Scrape egg white into egg yolk mixture with rubber spatula. Mix thoroughly with whisk. Add vanilla and beat with whisk. Let stand **15 minutes** (_____). Beat again with whisk and pour into large dessert dish or two 6-oz. custard cups. Top with cherry. Serve warm or cold.

DESSERTS

HONEY-GLAZED APPLE

4-oz. apple

Remove skin and core of apple with peeler/corer. Place apple in 1½-pint Menu-ette.

2½ tbsp. water
2 tbsp. honey
1/8 tsp. grated lemon peel
1 drop red food coloring

Mix remaining ingredients in custard cup. Pour over apple. Cover Menu-ette with lid. Cook **3 minutes (_____)** **at 100% power,** basting apple with liquid after each minute of cooking time. Baste several times with liquid while apple is cooling. To serve, put apple and 1 tbsp. liquid in dessert bowl.

APPLE CRISP

5-oz. apple

Peel apple, cut into quarters, remove core, and cut into 1/4-inch slices. Place on paper plate and cover with paper towel. Cook **2 minutes (_____) at 100% power,** giving plate a half-turn halfway through cooking time. (Auto-rotating oven: Eliminate turn.) Set aside.

3 tbsp. graham cracker crumbs
2 tbsp. all-purpose flour
2 tbsp. firmly packed dark brown sugar
4 tsp. butter

Combine graham cracker crumbs, flour, and sugar in 1½-pint mixing bowl. Cut in butter with pastry blender. Set aside 3 tbsp. of mixture in custard cup. Place remaining mixture in Corning Ware Petite Pan and press it against sides and bottom to form crust. Cook **30 seconds (_____) at 100% power.** Set aside.

1 oz. grated cheddar cheese
1 tbsp. chopped walnuts

Put cheese, nuts, and cooked apple into emptied mixing bowl. Mix thoroughly and place mixture in pan. Top with reserved dry mixture. Cook **1 minute (_____) at 100% power.** Turn pan halfway around. Cook **50 seconds (_____) at 100% power.** (Auto-rotating oven: Eliminate turn.) Set aside on counter for **5 minutes (_____)** to cool. Serve warm or cold.

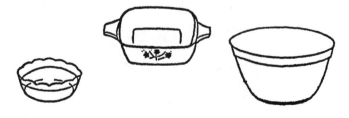

PEACH SOUFFLE

1 tbsp. water
1 tbsp. sugar
1/4 tsp. unflavored gelatin
dash of nutmeg
dash of salt

Combine water, sugar, gelatin, nutmeg, and salt in 1-cup liquid measure. Cook **15 seconds (_____) at 100% power** until gelatin dissolves.

1 small egg, separated
1/2 tsp. lemon juice
1/16 tsp. vanilla
1 drop almond extract

Put egg white into 2-cup liquid measure and set aside. Put egg yolk into custard cup and gradually add hot gelatin mixture, stirring continuously with small wire whisk. When mixed, return mixture to liquid measure. Add lemon juice and stir. Cook **30 seconds (_____) at 100% power** until mixture thickens. Stir in vanilla and almond extract and set aside.

4-oz. ripe peach

Peel peach. Cut in half all around pit and twist halves in opposite directions. Pit should then be easy to remove and discard. Dice peach and add half to gelatin mixture. Stir. Refrigerate **15 minutes (_____)** until set.

1 tbsp. heavy cream

Beat egg white with electric mixer until stiff. Place cream in clean 1-cup liquid measure and beat until stiff with only one beater attached to electric mixer. Add cream and remaining diced peach to egg white and mix with rubber spatula. Refrigerate until gelatin mixture is ready.
Remove both chilled mixtures from refrigerator. Mix together with rubber spatula and pour into 6- or 8-oz. custard cup. Chill **30 minutes (_____)** before serving.

RHUBARB CRISP

6 oz. rhubarb

Wash rhubarb and cut into 1/4-inch slices. Pack down into 16-oz. ceramic souffle dish and set aside.

3 tbsp. quick-cooking oats
1/4 cup firmly packed
** light brown sugar**
1/4 cup all-purpose flour
1/8 tsp. salt
1/4 tsp. cinnamon
2 tbsp. butter

Place remaining ingredients in 1-quart mixing bowl. Cut in butter with pastry blender until mixture is thoroughly blended. Pour over rhubarb and pack down with rubber spatula. Cook **6 minutes** (_____) **at 100% power,** giving dish a quarter-turn after each **1:30 minutes**(_____). (Autorotating oven: Eliminate turns.) Let cool **15 minutes** (_____) before serving.

INDEX

Gruyere cheese
  See Cheese, Gruyere

Half and Half
  asparagus soup, 27
  cheese 'n' egg, 55
  cheese soup, 28
  cucumber soup, 29
  flounder Swiss, 126
  shrimp soup, 34
  stuffed baked potato, 94
  tomato soup, 35
  Tracy's favorite seafood muffin, 141
Ham
  and asparagus omelet, 59
  and cheese sandwich, 42
  and eggs, 23
  slice, 179
Hamburger, 47
  See also Burger
Honey-glazed apple, 245
Hot cereal, 13
Hot cocoa, 192
Hot cocoa and marshmallows, 192
Hot dog, 46
  and sauerkraut, 46
  beans and franks, 183
  cheese and franks, 183
  cheese hot dog, 46
Hot orange drink, 191
Hot spiced wine, 192
Hungarian bacon and tomatoes, 180

Icing
  See Frosting
Instant cheese sauce, 107
Irish coffee with whipped cream, 193
Irish whiskey
  Irish coffee with whipped cream, 193
Italian cheesecake, 204
Italian plum preserves, 112
Italian sausage
  See Sausage, Italian

Italian steak, 162

Kingfish steak, 128

Ladyfingers, 220
Lamb
  breast of, Momma's, 173
  chop, 172
  pattie, 172
Langostinos, 34
Lasagna, easy (mafalda), 70
Leftover
  meat stew, 163
  spice cake, 212
Lemon-batter fish, 122
Lemon cake, 209
Lemon juice
  baked shrimp, 134
  breaded fish, Momma's, 120
  broccoli, 85
  cheesecake, 203
  cottage cheese pie, 226
  hot spiced wine, 192
  lemon cake, 209
  lemon pudding, 237
  lemon wafers, 221
  lemon-batter fish, 122
  lobster tail, 131
  marmalade, 114
  old-fashioned bread pudding, 231
  peach souffle, 247
  southern barbecue sauce, 106
  spicy barbecue sauce, 105
  stuffed cabbage, 146
Lemon peel
  cottage cheese pie, 226
  honey-glazed apple, 245
  lemon cake, 209
  lemon pudding, 237
  lemon wafers, 221
  marmalade, 114
Lemon pudding, 237
Lemon wafers, 221